Frank Buchman's Secret

FRANK BUCHMAN

Peter Howard

FRANK BUCHMAN'S SECRET

DOUBLEDAY & COMPANY, INC.
Garden City, New York

Library of Congress Catalog Card Number 62–15095

Printed in the United States of America
First Edition in the United States of America

Contents

1 *Spur in Our Flank* 9
2 *Revolutionary Road* 19
3 *Not Left, not Right, but Straight* 33
4 *"Fire from Heaven"* 50
5 *Africa with an Answer* 59
6 *Who Changes Hate, Changes History* 69
7 *America Needs an Ideology* 81
8 *The Result is a Miracle* 98
9 *Cabinets Must Learn this Art* 112
10 *Future Leadership* 125
11 *Brave Men Choose* 139

Frank Buchman's Secret

ONE

Spur in Our Flank

There was a secret in Frank Buchman's life. Now the world must know it.

It brought him love and hate. It led him to believe that everyone he met, rich and poor, black and white, boss and worker, could and should be made new. It bore him to the heart of nations.

It made him think and live in global terms. The last challenge he gave, a few hours before he died, was, "I want to see the world governed by men governed by God. Why not let God run the whole world?" Forty-five years before, in 1916, he was telling a group of men and women, who did not fully understand what he was saying, "I want you to live for continents. I want you to think for continents."

It made him a spur in the flank of our times. A German newspaper, the *Frankfurter Allgemeine Zeitung*, called him "the conscience of the world." The Prime Minister of New Zealand, Mr. Holyoake, says "Buchman has done as much as any man of our time to unite the peoples of the world by cutting through the prejudices of color, class and creed." And Sayadaw U Narada, Secretary of the Presiding Abbots' Association of Burma, who traveled 6000 miles with four other senior abbots to meet him, said, "Such a man comes once in a thousand years to show humanity the right way."

The aim of this book is truth, not praise.

What manner of man was Frank Buchman?

In Milan a few months before he died, he was talking early in the morning to some friends. A newspaper on the other side of the world had attacked him. Frank Buchman said, "I do not say I am without sin. I do say I live for one thing only: to make Jesus Christ regnant in the life of every person I meet—including the man who is going to bring me my breakfast."

There were three barmen at the hotel. Frank Buchman did not buy drink from them. He went into their bar, and gave them the bread of life. They and their families all found something new from their friendship with him. One of them said of him, "Dr. Buchman is different from most of the people I see. We have cleaned things up here since he came. Most of the leaders of Italy come to this bar sooner or later. The Foreign Minister was here the other day. He was so interested in what we told him about Buchman that he almost forgot his drink."

These men, and hundreds of men like them, became part of the revolution Buchman was bringing at that time to Sesto san Giovanni, the steel city outside Milan. It is a place where hate reigns in thousands of hearts. There is poverty and injustice. Not many years ago workers were shot in the streets and bosses were thrown alive into the steel furnaces. Others were smashed to death with trucks in the factory yard. All night long, in winter, the hammer and sickle glows red above the doors of hundreds of Communist homes.

But that Christmas, the Communist Mayor of Sesto lent the principal Communist hall for a dinner given by the citizens of Sesto to hear the news of Frank Buchman's work and to meet some of the men, Communist and non-Communist, Christian and non-Christian, who had begun to change and to live to remake the world.

That year a crib and Christmas tree stood in the heart of that Communist stronghold.

Some months before he died, Frank Buchman visited Oxford. He sat talking with his old friend Sir Richard Livingstone, once Vice-Chancellor of the University and an educator of world-wide reputation.

Livingstone had followed his work for years. The old friends talked that day of the miracles in men that had happened in the University. When Frank Buchman had first come to Oxford in 1921, the news reached a leading atheist in the University. His father was a clergyman. He was a brilliant student. He was appointed a lecturer before he took his final examinations.

He held public meetings on Sunday afternoons. He asked well-known Christians to argue the case for Christianity. Then he put the case for atheism, called for a show of hands, and always won.

Someone told the atheist that Frank Buchman believed in the Holy Spirit. He thought that was nonsense. So he decided to ask Buchman to his rooms for coffee after dinner and argue him out of his beliefs. For an hour he gave his arguments for atheism. Buchman sat there nodding his head, saying, "Really?" and "Very interesting."

A tennis player can go on serving at tennis as long as he

has any tennis balls. If his opponent refuses to knock them back over the net, the game cannot go on. This is what happened that night. After an hour the atheist saw that he was not getting anywhere. He suddenly said to Frank Buchman, "I wish you would tell me what you think of me."

Buchman answered, "You don't want me to be rude, do you?" The atheist persisted. So Buchman said, "I feel three things about you. First, you are unhappy."

The other answered, "Yes, I am."

Buchman said, "You have a very unhappy home."

The atheist answered, "Yes, I have. I hate my father. I always have since I was a boy."

Buchman then said, "You are in the grip of an impure habit which you cannot bring yourself to talk about with anyone."

The atheist answered, "That is a lie." There was silence.

Buchman said, "I must go."

The atheist said, "Please stay."

Buchman said, "I must go."

"No, don't go."

Buchman then said, "Well, I'll stay on one condition—that you and I listen to God together."

The atheist made a surprising reply. He said, "I couldn't do that. I told you a lie a few minutes ago. I am in the grip of that habit."

Buchman said, "I know." The men talked honestly together. They ended the evening on their knees. The atheist said, "I want to give my life to God." And he did so.

Next day he wrote a letter of apology to his father. He also went to the professor with whom he had been working on a book about atheism. He put the manuscript on the professor's table and said, "Well, we'll have to scrap all that."

The professor said, "Why?"

The former atheist said, "We are for truth. The truth is that God has come into my life as a reality."

The professor took another puff at his pipe and said, "Well, I suppose we will have to scrap it." The whole manuscript went into the wastepaper basket.

At Cambridge a few weeks later the man who had been an atheist stood up and told a number of people, "Whatever I may have said before, I can never deny that here we have stood together in the presence of God."

Livingstone talked over many such stories with Frank Buchman on that last visit to Oxford. Then he said, "When you and I were young there were moral fences along the road of life. We did not always keep to them. But we knew when we crossed them. Today all the moral fences are down. And look at the world. Your job is to build those fences anew."

Livingstone said that today the problem is not just that men are against moral standards, but that they no longer believe there is any such thing as good and evil, right and wrong. He spoke of promiscuity and perversion in the University. Then, talking of the days when he was head of an Oxford College, he said to Frank Buchman, "You saw much more than I did about where the wrong lay. And you were able to cure it. I would like to be able to do that." "You can," said Buchman. He began to tell Livingstone how to help other men become new.

After Livingstone said goodbye, Buchman asked to see the woman who had helped to keep his hotel room clean. She came from the North Country, a typical miner's daughter, now nearing middle age—genuine, large, comfortable, shrewd. When she was inside the room, he asked her to sit down. For more than half an hour he talked with her, pouring out the best of his heart and life. He could have given no more had she been the pivot of some great nation. Outside the door again, she said, "I have been in service for twenty-five years. It is the first time that any guest at any hotel I worked in ever asked to talk to me as a friend. It made me feel as if I counted. I see I can do something in the world as well as keep rooms clean. It has made me very happy."

A few weeks later Frank Buchman made a speech based on his talk with Livingstone. It was a sign of the world's hunger for an answer that this speech was broadcast in thirty-six languages by Rome Radio, in twenty languages, including Chinese, from Tokyo, and by the sixteen French-speaking radio stations of Africa. Newspapermen calculate that the speech was carried by press, radio and television to over one thousand million people.

Once Buchman arrived in England and went to his London home. The people who had been acting as host and hostess in his absence were giving a dinner party, and some of the leading political figures of the day were coming to the house that evening. When Buchman heard this, he sent for the host and hostess of the dinner and said to them, "I want you to know that you never have to feel I must be at table when I am in this house. I want to be there if I can help you with your friends, but never feel obliged to include me."

Part of Frank Buchman's secret, which made so many say that their meeting with him was a turning point in their life, was his belief that he did nothing. God did everything if you allowed Him to do so. A Scottish coal miner, Peter

O'Conner, went to see him. He met a man who loved him, understood his failures and needs, and helped him to find the will and way to live his best. O'Connor said, "In my half-hour with you, I was helped more than by any other living soul."

Buchman answered, "It is not my art. It is God's art."

A few years ago, when Frank Buchman was ill and in pain, hundreds of people were coming from every part of the world to an assembly at Mackinac Island, Michigan. Buchman spent the day before they arrived going to every room where they would sleep, with a list of the guests in his hand. He said, "We must do our best for every one of them. I am going to see myself that everything is right." By the evening he was grey with tiredness. He had to be helped to bed. For an hour he lay in silence, while the sun set and the stars came out above the waters of the Great Lakes where the long boats carry the ore through the straits to the mills of the Middle West.

Suddenly he said, "We are on the eve of a very great advance." A friend sitting in his room and surprised at these words, asked why he said them. Buchman answered, "I am absolutely helpless. I could not even turn over in bed without someone to lift me. I can do nothing. Again and again before a great advance I have found that God makes me feel like this, so that I never forget He does everything, and I do nothing." After a minute he said, "I'd like to pray. Jesus, make me a better man. And thank you for the pain, which, taken in the right spirit, purifies and strengthens. Amen."

In the last year of his life, a European Cabinet Minister, whose hands held power in much of the trade and cash of the Continent, came to see him. This man spoke of the way in which he had seen the tide of Communism turned in the Ruhr. He spoke of how in four years the Communist vote in the Works Councils there fell from 72 per cent to 8 per cent.

He recalled the words of a Japanese Prime Minister who had told the Press that men trained by Frank Buchman had saved his country from dictatorship and Communism in 1960. Then he said, "You must feel very proud of all this."

Buchman answered, "I do not feel that way at all. I have had nothing to do with it. God does everything. I only obey and do what He says." The Cabinet Minister said, "Oh, I cannot accept that. You yourself have done great things." Buchman replied, "I have done nothing. Or rather, I have been doing what men like yourself should have been doing all the time. I stopped trying to run things the way I wanted, many years ago. I started listening to God and letting Him have His way in everything. If men like you did that, you would find the answers, instead of spending your lives beaten by the problems you yourselves create."

Frank Buchman told that statesman that the only way to answer the needs of nations was by a change in men. He repeated the words of the late Lord Salisbury who said in the House of Lords, "What we need are God-guided personalities, to make God-guided nationalities, to make a new world." When King George VI heard of Lord Salisbury's interest in Frank Buchman's work he sent someone to ask why. Salisbury said, "I saw the Spirit of God moving on the waters, and I dare not stand aside."

It was Carl Hambro, the man who was President of the League of Nations during its heyday and at last laid it to rest when it failed, who said at Geneva to Frank Buchman, "You have created that constructive peace which we have been seeking in vain for years. Where we have failed in changing politics, you have succeeded in changing lives."

And to the last hours of his life people around him changed.

A girl was helping to look after his room in the hotel in Freudenstadt where he died.

The hotel lies in the Black Forest. It is in the woods there that he walked one day in 1938, along the path now called Frank Buchmanweg, and had the clear thought: "Moral and spiritual re-armament. The next great movement in the world will be a movement of moral re-armament for all nations."

This girl was so polished and painted that you could hardly see her real face or eyelashes. She marvelled to learn that this man of eighty-three knew her home town, knew the King of her country, and the previous King, his father.

Someone gave her a copy of Frank Buchman's speeches. She read them. Frank Buchman asked her if she liked her job. She replied, "No. I hate hard work, and they make us work hard here. I want to be an air hostess."

He told the girl of how God had a full plan for her life, and that if she listened to Him, He would tell her what it was.

Soon afterward he fell ill and died. A few days later a friend went to tidy his room. He went inside. There, kneeling beside the bed, was this girl and another, a friend of hers. They were praying.

She stood up. Her face was her own and her eyes were alight. She said, "That man was nearly four times my age. He did not say much to me. But keeping this room clean has been an experience that will last all through my life. I found a faith in God because I understood what he was living for. I shall never be the same again."

TWO

Revolutionary Road

Moscow Radio again and again attacks the work of Frank Buchman. In one broadcast it said, "Moral Re-Armament is a global ideology with bridgeheads in every continent, now in its final phase of total expansion throughout the world. It has the power to capture radical, revolutionary minds." Buchman himself believed the need of the age to be "the greatest revolution of all time whereby the Cross of Christ will transform the world."

Sometimes people got angry that he would not do things the way they wished. A Protestant Bishop once scolded him for not talking enough about Christ in one of his public speeches. Buchman replied, "I'm sorry I did not please you. I will try to do better. But as you have told me what is on your mind, I will be honest with you. I came to see you the other day. You welcomed me. You gave me coffee. But I was surprised that you never once told me you loved your wife."

The Bishop stared at Buchman with full-moon eyes. Buchman waited a moment then said, "It is not always essential to tell everybody the thing most deeply in your heart the first time you meet them."

People will never understand the secret of Frank Buchman unless they judge him as a revolutionary. That is what he was. He did not look at life or people through the same eyes as those of other men. He did not think of people as black, white, brown or yellow, but as sons of God with the same needs which the same answer could meet. He said, "It is not a question of color, but of character." And in 1915, on the first of his many visits to Asia, he said, "Crows are black the whole world over," meaning that human nature is everywhere the same.

He did not think of people as of different classes. He did not lick the boots of Kings—nor did he possess that proletarian snobbery which treats such men with scorn because they are born of royal blood.

He did not think that a man was a better or worse man because of his wealth—or lack of it. He sympathized with poor men and did his best to help them materially and in every way—but he was far from that patronage of poverty which refuses to face the need of the poor for the same honesty and purity that the world rightly demands from the rich. Challenged once that Moral Re-Armament was a "class movement," he replied instantly. "That is so. We believe there are two classes in the world—men who change and those who refuse to do so."

He said, "There is enough in the world for everybody's need but not for everybody's greed. If everybody cared enough, and everybody shared enough, wouldn't everybody have enough?"

He lived that spirit and saw that those around him lived it too. For the last forty years of his life he had no salary and no assured income of any kind. He went in the faith that "Where God guides, he will provide." He spent nothing on himself except for essential service such as buying clothes, travelling from place to place, getting his hair cut and his shoes mended. He never owned a motor car. And the only property that was his was the family home in Allentown, Pennsylvania, where his mother and father lived and died. He shared all he was given with those who needed it.

During the depression of the 'thirties, a British leader of the unemployed came to see Buchman. He was bitter about the state of his class, envious of those richer than he and suspicious that Buchman was a tool of his class enemies. Buchman listened to him—and was moved by his passion and his poverty. They listened to God together. Buchman said, "I have guidance to give you half of all I have." He went to a drawer and took out his bank-book. He showed the unemployed leader what he had—an amazingly small sum for one responsible for a world force—and gave him a check for half of it. He emptied his pockets and gave him half of that too. Together, it came to nine pounds. "Now we are both Socialists," said Buchman with a smile. "Of course," commented the unemployed leader afterward, "he knows there is far more to Socialism than dividing your wallet with your neighbor. But it was his gracious way of helping me to accept a gift which at that time he felt guided by God to give me." The unemployed man changed, and worked with Buchman for life.

When a friend of his was worried about money, Buchman said to him, "I cannot understand you. You puzzle me. I began with two or three people. Since that time, God has taken this work to scores of nations and to millions of people throughout the world. It is growing all the time. We have never had debts. We have never had assured sources of income. God has never left us without provision. Why should He begin to do so now?"

Buchman was meticulous with money, accounting for every penny, never letting a letter be posted if it could be delivered. He hated waste. But he never let the cost of a venture be the deciding factor. He would carefully test whether it was right, and if so go forward in faith. He would send 250 people, with equipment for two plays, on a 35,000-mile journey round the world, even though he did not have the resources to finance them, strong in the faith that God would provide for every need as they went. In fifty years he never had much to spare, but always enough for what he had to do.

When newspapermen in Bombay were throwing questions in his face, like stones, about the mysterious American millionaires and tycoons who were supposed to be giving him money, he told the truth. He said that Moral Re-Armament is financed by thousands of gifts, rarely large ones, not from surplus but from sacrifice, by those who are convinced of the need of this answer. Afterward, speaking of those who suggested that he was being financed by big industry, he said with a smile, "Sometimes I almost wish it were true."

Once he had been given such a chance. One of the wealthiest men of America, perceiving Buchman's power to change men, asked him to be the head of a great organization of his creating. He offered Buchman palatial headquarters, a staff of workers, almost unlimited finance. But it was clear to Buchman that if this man financed him he would, in fact, want to use his money to control what Buchman did. Buchman refused. It was then made plain to him that if he did not accept, steps would be taken to prevent his receiving money from any American philanthropist. Buchman's guidance was, "I must obey God not man. He will provide."

Four landmarks in Frank Buchman's life marked his early road to revolution.

The first was in 1908. As a young man, he had been accused by a friend of ambition. Stung by this, he began to work in the most difficult part of Philadelphia, looking after under-privileged boys. To start with, they lived in a room above a stable. The smell of horses came up through the floor. The boys were difficult—"little wild men" Buchman called them. He used to get them down to breakfast on time on Sundays, not by scolding, but by having pancakes on the table. He learned there a lesson which lasted through life—never to be shocked at other people's failings and never to laugh at other people's faults "because you are just as funny yourself." The venture grew into a hospice, later adopted in other cities, and a settlement house.

A committee of six men controlled the money on which this enterprise depended. When the money was short, the committee decided to cut down the food the boys ate. The boys were hungry. Buchman was angry. He was awake all night brooding in bitterness. In the morning he did not come down to breakfast, and a friend found him in bed, still racked with frustration and fury. That day he resigned his job. But his feelings were so deep that he fell ill. He consulted a specialist who told him to take a hot and a cold bath each day and he would feel better. He took baths as suggested for six months. He became one of the cleanest men in the world outside, but felt no better inside. His organization, which had seemed so successful, was thwarted. He was hurt. He hated. His health cracked under the strain of his bitterness.

Here, in the words he used over thirty years ago, is the story of this experience:

"I failed. I said the Committee were behaving badly. Yet my work had become my idol. All I should have done was to resign and let it go at that. Right in my conviction, I was wrong in harboring ill-will. I left and came abroad. En route I had the vision of 'Care' in Horace's Ode, following me on a charger, always just behind. I could almost hear the horse's hoofs and feel its breath on the back of my neck.

"Travelling through Italy and other parts of the Continent, I found my way back to England, and so up to Keswick, where a convention was in progress. And there something happened. Something for which I shall always be grateful."

At Keswick he went one Sunday to a church. Only seventeen people were there. A woman was talking about the Cross of Christ. "She unravelled the Cross for me," he said. "A doctrine which I knew as a boy, which my Church believed, which I had always taught, that day became a great reality for me. I had entered the little church with a divided will, nursing pride, selfishness, ill-will. The woman's simple talk personalized the Cross for me that day, and suddenly I had a poignant vision of the Crucified. I thought of those six committee men. I was the seventh wrong man.

"With this deeper experience of how the love of God in Christ had bridged the chasm dividing me from Him, and the new sense of buoyant life that had come, I returned to the house feeling a powerful urge to share my experience. Thereupon I wrote to the six committee men in America against whom I had nursed ill-will and told them my experience, and how at the foot of the Cross I could only think of my own sin. At the top of each letter I wrote this verse:

When I survey the wondrous Cross
On which the Prince of Glory died,
My richest gain I count but loss,
And pour contempt on all my pride.

"Then I said,

My dear Friend,

I have nursed ill-will against you. I am sorry. Forgive me?

Yours sincerely,

FRANK"

At the age of over eighty-one, just eighteen months before he died, Frank Buchman was talking to some friends and again spoke of the experience at Keswick. Here are some of the things he said.

"Today I was carried back in memory to Keswick on that Sunday afternoon where seventeen people were gathered. I saw Christ on the Cross. 'This hast Thou done for me; What have I done for Thee, Thou Crucified?'

Thou of life the Fountain art;
Freely let me take of Thee,
Spring Thou up within my heart,
Rise to all eternity.

"And there came in my life a vivid sense of having experienced the Atonement. And I left that service with a consciousness of having the complete answer to all my difficulties and sins. I heard the wind of heaven. It passed over me and through me, and I walked out of that place a different man.

"When I went out I met a young man, just a gay young blade. He was with his family who lived in the next house to us on the hill overlooking Derwentwater. And he said, 'How about a walk?' And I said, 'All right.' And we walked around Derwentwater. I told him my experience—what I had seen at that service and how that revelation of the Cross of Christ met my instant need. And before we had reached the end, he, too, had an experience. He was a fresher at Cambridge, and he went and told his father and mother. Of course, they were overjoyed. That was in 1908.

"It is fifty-one years ago that that experience came to me. It made all the difference in the world.

At the Cross, at the Cross, where I first saw the light,
  And the burden of my sin rolled away;
It was there by faith I received my sight,
  And now I am happy all the day.

"That put order into my life.

"I feel a great many people speak of the Cross, but it does not mean a thing. It isn't real. It is something they hear about or read about, something somebody else has. But an *experience* of the Cross is vital, real, and goes straight into your life.

"You remember the experience of Paul, what happened to him on the Damascus Road. Paul heard a voice, but saw no man, and he was transformed. It is this kinship with the heavenly force which brings that alignment, as we listen to the still, small Voice.

"With an experience of the Cross, you will shrink from nothing. I learned at Keswick that I was as wrong as anybody else. I was most in need of change. I was the one to begin."

A second landmark in his life was at State College, Pennsylvania. Soon after the experience at Keswick, the Chairman of the Democratic National Committee of the United States asked Buchman to go there. The Chairman was on the Board of Trustees of the college and he was worried. For the college was a problem. Students were on strike against their teachers. Drunkenness had become fashionable. Although the place was supposed to be "dry," nineteen drinking parties were taking place the night Buchman arrived. As he told the story later, "There was enough liquor to float a battleship."

Buchman saw that the three men who held the key to the life of that college were the Dean, an agnostic; a popular student called Blair Buck, son of a Judge of the Supreme Court of Montana, who described himself as a Confucianist but had no real faith; and William Gilliland, who looked after the horses of the local doctor by day and smuggled drink into the students' quarters at night. He had been given the nickname Bill Pickle.

These three men changed. Through their change, the spirit of the whole place was transformed. It become a model of Christian education. Twelve hundred men out of the sixteen hundred at that time in the college came to Bible classes each week. The Catholic priest held what he called "Frank Buchman Masses" for lapsed Catholics who returned to the Church as a result of his work. People came from far and near to see what wonders God had wrought.[1]

For the remaining twenty years of his life, Bill Pickle worked with Buchman. At the age of eighty he went with Buchman to Geneva and spoke to leaders of the League of

[1] For this story see *Remaking the World* by Frank N. D. Buchman (1961 edition), pp. 330–46.

Nations there. Blair Buck laid the foundation for much of the educational work among the Negroes of the Southern States of America. His influence was such that the transition in race relations took place naturally and peaceably in areas where violence had been foreseen. Fifty-four years after they first met, when Frank Buckman died, Blair Buck and his wife were travelling with an international force of Moral Re-Armament in Peru. Children of Bill Pickle came to Buchman's funeral in 1961 and told how the faith their father had found more than half a century before was now passed on to his grandchildren.

At Penn State, Frank Buchman learned the secret of full obedience to the Voice of God. Here in his own words are some of the lessons which, learned between 1908 and 1915, lasted all his life.

"I was so busy with people coming to make appointments with me that I had to have two telephones in my room. Still I was dissatisfied with the results. So I decided on a radical procedure—to give that hour of the day between five and six in the morning, when the phones were unlikely to ring, to listen to the still, small Voice to inspire and direct. God told me what to do and I wrote it down. There is no virtue about writing it down, but I have a treacherous memory. It is just like a sieve. Everything goes through and I forget; so I write it down. If you have a memory that keeps things in a photographic way, you are to be complimented, but I am a stupid man and I have to write them down. The Chinese tell us that the strongest memory is weaker than the palest ink."

It was Frank Buchman's quality of listening that later struck observers. Herbert Grevenius wrote in *Stockholms-Tidningen* in 1938: "It is not Frank Buchman's lightning smile that forms his secret. His epigrammatic sayings, his power to hold an assembly in his hand and yet submerge himself—none of these tells you anything about Frank Buchman. Look closely at his pictures and you will see something in his expression, a sort of listening. Sit a few days and study his face, and you will be amazed how often he appears almost at a loss, not to say helpless. He makes no secret of it. There is one basis only to his fabulously active life—guidance, for which he is openly on the watch every moment. He is a sail always held to be filled by the wind, a man with a great and warm and humble heart, a democrat out to make men free under the dictatorship of God."

Another newspaper editor wrote: "It is impossible to understand him unless he is thought of as always in God's presence, listening for direction and accepting power, which he says is the normal way for any sane human being to live."

"I learned another thing at State College," Buchman said. "When Bill peddled liquor to these students I often saw them carried down at night. I have seen real catastrophe in the lives of students, and I say, very sincerely and very bluntly, it's a hell of a life if you don't have the Gospel of Jesus Christ. There is only one thing which is adequate and it is Someone who can change you, Someone who loves you. If you have this power, men and women will come to you night and day for an answer. All sorts of people.

"This is an art everyone wants to learn, and heaven help us if we don't learn it. We need to learn it for the sake of our own children. Your own children must come and tell you about themselves and you will be honest with them because you know what a rascal you were yourself. That is the way to win your children, and that is the reason why this crowd of youth flocks around us now. They will go to a man who understands them, who doesn't talk too good or appear too wise, a man who is honest about himself."

It was in those far-off years, too, that Frank Buchman learned the importance of discipline in his own life if he wanted to help others find an answer to defeat in theirs. He used to say of the standards of absolute honesty, absolute purity, absolute unselfishness and absolute love: "Those are Christ's standards. Are they yours?" But he did not make rules for other people. He described Moral Re-Armament as a "lake in which lambs can wade and elephants can swim." He once said, "There is a certain level of Moral Re-Armament in everybody. Our job is to raise the level."

But the tragedy of drink in the life of men like Bill Pickle made a print in his heart that lasted. Bill Pickle used to say that if Buchman or those working with him had taken even one drop of drink when they first got to know him, he would never have been won to a faith in God that became the helm and sail of his course in life. Frank Buchman put it in these words, "Now I've been reared in circumstances where I could have liquor all my life and whenever I wanted it. But there's one reason why I don't touch a drop. It is because of fellows like Bill Pickle. You don't win them if you touch a drop, just that cocktail. I don't tell anybody else not to drink. Anybody can do anything he wants. Everybody has the liberty of the Spirit, but for my part, I think of men like Bill.

"It's exactly the same with smoking. I don't smoke, but I don't say it's wrong for you. I couldn't do it, because Bill in the old days was a regular chain smoker. When he changed, everything just dropped off. No smoking, no drinking, although I never said anything to him about it. It is amazing how these—I won't call them sins, I just call them nice little vices—can sometimes be the key to a man's whole life."

Buchman believed that it was a question of whether you were trying to please yourself or to help others. He often told the story of a friend from Scotland who had led, as he felt, a blameless life but who never was used by God to bring change to another person. Through his friendship with Frank Buchman he became a man of effective faith and used to say, "In the old days, my friends could never make me drunk—but I could never make them sober."

Buchman made many angry with his belief, "If you are not winning, you are sinning," by which he meant that if you were not living in such a way that people around you found in you the answer to the fears, hates and impurities of their lives, there was something wrong with you.

Another landmark happened during a journey by train in the year 1912. It was in Canada. Suddenly there came to him, with a sense of special insight, the conviction that Christianity has a moral backbone. He saw clearly that the reason why so many Christians were well-meaning but powerless in the lives of their nations and even their families was because they professed Christ with their lips but compromised in their lives. He saw that any valid experience of faith carried deep moral change with it. He saw that those who professed faith but lived filth, denied before men the power of God as a force in their nature.

One of the mightiest landmarks in Frank Buchman's life was in 1921. He had been invited to Washington by a senior British officer attending the Disarmament Conference. He saw then what so few perceived—that the world was not just at the end of a great war but at the start of a breakdown of civilization, where every moral value so far accepted by man would be challenged and denied.

At that time, this British officer sent him a postcard with the picture of a man's head on it. Underneath was the sentence, "God gave a man two ears and one mouth. Why not listen twice as much as you talk?"

As Frank Buchman journeyed to Washington by train through the night listening to the clang of the wheels and also to the voice in his heart, one thought came clearly to him, "Resign, resign, resign." It meant giving up the safe, salaried position which he then held at a New England college. By the time he reached Washington, he had decided. He resigned and never again held a salaried position until his life's end. He cut his bonds with human security and put his trust in God alone.

He went to Europe. One moonlit night he was in Petty Cury, Cambridge. His spirit was overwhelmed with the vastness of the world's need—the moral landslide of nations, the hate and fears that war had multiplied, the flight from faith, the dalliance with doubt which decadence in the home had created, the rising force of world Communism. Suddenly, as he faced the truth about what needed to be done, the thought struck strongly into his heart: "*You will be used to remake the world.*"

He quailed at this. The thought so overwhelmed him that for three days he told nobody. He would not write down the thought, though for many years he had formed the habit of putting down on paper the thoughts that came to him as he listened. But the idea came to him again and again. He knew he could not do it—but he also believed God could do anything in, by, with, through and for a man wholly given to His will.

At last he accepted this guidance as a challenge and a calling.

A little later, in a room at Oxford University, he sat with two or three friends. He said to them, "We are few. But if we stick together and do only those things which, so far as God shows us, we believe He wants us to do, we shall be used together to remake the thinking and living of the world."

These decisions turned Buchman from a man of faith into a man of ideological force. They gave him an outlook on events and a vision for men and nations that affected modern history.

A diplomat who, for a quarter of a century, has had to negotiate with the Russians and others at most of the post-war conferences, gave this verdict on Buchman: "He has done three things. He saw the real problem many years before the rest of us understood it. He forged an answer out of human lives that cured the problem. He then did the hardest job of all—he built a force of people in every continent who are bringing that answer to the world."

THREE

Not Left, not Right, but Straight

Frank Buchman possessed the genius of continuance. When he made friends with somebody, it was a friendship that lasted into the third and fourth generations. He paid his first of many visits to Asia in 1915. In Japan, Baron Shibusawa, founder of modern Japanese industry, was his host. Today Baron Shibusawa's great-great-grandchildren play their part in the remaking of the world.

In that same year Mahatma Gandhi became a friend of Buchman's and it was a friendship that lasted through life. The Mahatma said that Moral Re-Armament was "the best thing that has come out of the West." His son, Devadas Gandhi, publisher and editor of the *Hindustan Times,* said, "If Moral Re-Armament fails, the world fails." Manilal Gandhi, editor of *Indian Opinion,* the newspaper founded by his father in South Africa, published a special number of which the theme was: "Moral Re-Armament is creating a new dimension of racial unity in South Africa." Rajmohan Gandhi, the grandson, left his newspaper career a few years ago. His life is now given to bringing the message of Moral Re-Armament to the nations of the world.

Frank Buchman's secret of friendship was that he swiftly went to the root and heart of life with people. Lord Lytton, who as acting-Viceroy of India welcomed Frank Buchman's friendship and entertained him on several occasions, said in the last year of his life, "I owe more to my friendship with Frank Buchman than to that of any other living man." At a time when the British and the Indians were engaged in bitter controversy, Frank Buchman moved between the homes and families of the leaders of Congress and the Viceregal Palace, and enjoyed the confidence of both parties, in a way that was given to few other men.

Once he was having lunch with another Viceroy at the time of the Belgaum Conference. The Viceroy said, "Where have you been?" Buchman replied, "I have been at Belgaum." "Belgaum!" said the Viceroy. "I hope you did not meet the Ali brothers there? They are terrible people." The Ali brothers at that time were leading a movement in India which would have ended in an attempt to throw the British forcibly out of the country.

Frank Buchman replied, "Do you find them terrible? They are friends of mine." Then he went on with his lunch.

The Viceroy was interested. He spent some time explaining his own position, and then said, "What would you do if you were in my place?"

Buchman laid down his knife and fork and said, "Since you have asked me, I would treat the Ali brothers as you have treated me. You have been good to me. You invited me here and sat me at your right hand. I would do just the same to the Ali brothers."

The Viceroy was astounded and annoyed. But thinking it over, he did what had been suggested. The Ali brothers accepted his invitation and sat, one on his left side and one on his right. Later, with the Viceroy's blessing and backing, they were sent as delegates to the St. James's Palace Conference, which was a stage on the long road that ended in India's independence.

Lady Minto, wife of another Viceroy, also became a firm friend of Frank Buchman, as did her sister Lady Antrim. Today Lady Antrim's great-grandchildren, the fourth generation, are playing their part in Moral Re-Armament.

Lady Minto and Lady Antrim travelled with Frank Buchman in many parts of the world. While on a journey through the Middle East, they spent half a day on the island of Cyprus. There they took a taxi at Larnaca and drove into the countryside. Nearly twenty years later some British soldiers on the island met the taxi driver who had been at the wheel on that occasion. He told them how that one ride with Frank Buchman had changed the course of his life. At the time of the bloodshed on Cyprus, that taxi driver still met with British friends interested in Moral Re-Armament, and they worked together to play their part in bringing an answer.

In Madras, over twenty years after Frank Buchman had been in the city, a cloakroom attendant in one of the hotels there fell on the floor and embraced the feet of a man who knew Buchman, saying, "Where is the master? I often think of him. He helped me to find something in my life that has made me happy in my family through years of hardship, often without much to eat or work to do."

Forty years after Frank Buchman first met his grandfather, Rajmohan Gandhi was working as a newspaper man in Britain. He was so impressed by what he saw in Frank Buchman's work that he resigned his job and decided to make Moral Re-Armament his calling. One of the leaders of India urged him that his duty lay in the newspapers. Rajmohan replied, "When my grandfather came back to this country from South Africa as a lawyer, his family urged him to continue with his legal practice. Instead, he put aside his private plans in order to free our country. Now there is a bigger job than freeing one country. The job is to save the whole world from dictatorship, corruption and war. I am going to put Moral Re-Armament in first place."

More than a year later this same Indian leader was going out of a building with Rajmohan Gandhi. They called a taxi. Rajmohan stood aside to let the older man in first. But the older man insisted on Rajmohan going before him, saying, "I want you to go first to show you that you were right and I was wrong."

In 1960, President Prasad told Rajmohan and some of his friends, in his Palace in Delhi, that in his opinion the work that they were doing was the most important thing happening in the life of India today.

Rajmohan's change affected the life of his family. He says:

"My mother and brother came to the Moral Re-Armament Assembly at Caux in Switzerland. My brother was fifteen. He was eager to change. He decided to go through his life in the light of the four standards. He came and told his mother where he needed to change, and he told her that once he had brought his report card from school and was congratulated by everybody for getting 90 marks out of 100 in arithmetic. He said to his mother, 'Of course, I got only 9 and the zero was added by me.'

"Then my brother found a passion to save his country. He said, 'I am going to show the film *The Crowning Experience* to the President of India.' Now certain people felt he couldn't do it. At that time he was only fifteen. It seemed crazy.

"But he returned to India. He made telephone calls, wrote letters and within two weeks he showed *The Crowning Experience* to the President. Not only was the President there with his family, but also military men and cabinet ministers. My brother had become free to fight for his country."

In Calcutta, one of the richest men in India was shocked into reality by his meeting with Frank Buchman. He arrived at a time when Buchman was about to listen to God with a number of his friends. The Indian, a Marwari, sat in silence wondering what was happening. Presently Buchman broke the silence and said, "The only thought I had was 'Stop stealing.' I don't know what it means. It may mean my watch that somebody stole the other day. It may refer to myself, though it is some years since I stole anything. I just don't know what it means." At this point the Marwari rose and hurried from the room. Buchman said, "Who was that man? I wish somebody had introduced me to him. I would like to have met him." Next day the Marwari appeared and said, "I am amazed how Buchman knew my problem. I have been cheating the government on taxes for years." He sent in a check that morning for thousands of rupees to the Government. He entertained Frank Buchman and over two hundred of his friends to meet many of the business leaders of the city, and told them with a glad heart how he had decided to be honest in the future.

In China, in the year 1917, Sun Yat-sen was among those who became friends with Buchman. The two men used to meet in the cellar of a cement factory. There were three exits to the cellar and Sun Yat-sen at that time was on the run. He did not want to be in any place unless he could get out of it quickly, in any direction where safety lay. Sun Yat-sen said that his talks with Buchman had a profound influence on his life, for Buchman was, he said, "the only man who told me the truth about myself."

Another friend of his at this time was a rich lawyer and diplomat. The lawyer was a gambler. He invited Buchman to his home and offered him cocktails and cigarettes. Buchman refused. But he noticed that the lawyer's hands were stained with nicotine and that he shook and quivered, even when he was sitting in his chair drinking his cocktails. The men played a game of tennis together and the lawyer invited him to stay to dinner. There were thirty courses to that Chinese meal and the lawyer took a different wine with almost every course. Frank Buchman, in telling the story, always remembered the twenty-year-old eggs that tasted like cheese, the sea slugs, the raw fish flakes, the bird's-nest soup and finally the chrysanthemum leaves dipped in sweets of different kinds. At the end of the meal the lawyer was very unsteady and offered to send Frank Buchman home in a chair carried by six coolies. "It's interesting how often people project onto you the thing they most need themselves," Frank Buchman used to say as he remembered that evening in the lawyer's home, "I did not need the chair to carry me home. He certainly needed someone to carry him at the end of his dinner. But I gratefully agreed as I did not want to upset him that night."

The lawyer accepted Buchman's invitation to come to dinner with him on the following night. At dinner, Frank Buchman began to tell him about guidance from God. He told the story of how he was walking down the street one evening and clearly had the thought to speak to the man walking in front of him. He had the thought, "That man is in great need." Not being sure, however, he said to himself, "If that man stops at the next lamp-post I will speak to him." The man stopped. Buchman went up to him and said, "I felt I ought to speak to you. I thought you might need something." The man replied, "Of course I'm in need. God must have sent you to me. I have come out for fresh air. But I am in terrible trouble. My mother is inside that hospital down the street. She is dying. My seven brothers and sisters are at the hospital and I don't know what to do with them." The men went to the hospital together. They prayed together. The whole of that family became interested in the work Buchman was doing, and they kept in touch with him through the years.

The Chinese lawyer said to Frank Buchman, "Do you think God can speak to people like me?"

"Of course I do," answered Buchman.

A great storm arose. Buchman invited the lawyer to stay the night. The lawyer said, "My wife is waiting for me."

"You've often kept her waiting before this," said Buchman.

The lawyer smiled and agreed, but said the coolies must

get home. Frank Buchman reminded him that three coolies had recently been eaten by tigers in a valley nearby and he thought they would be glad to stay the night. The visitor agreed to stay.

Frank Buchman asked the lawyer to read his favorite chapter of the Bible to him. The lawyer could not think of what his chapter was, but took a lucky dip. He had the misfortune to find a chapter full of long names and "begats." Nevertheless, he read it through from start to finish. The men then prayed together and went to sleep. Next morning the lawyer suggested that it was reading the Bible that had made him so sleepy.

Buchman said, "Perhaps so. Shall we read another chapter?"

The lawyer quickly said, "You read this time." Buchman read him I Corinthians vi, verses 9–11.

The lawyer said, "I didn't know that was in the Bible. But it applies to me. I didn't want to stay last night with you because I can't sleep without dope. My doctor gives me a pill to send me to sleep and another pill to wake me up properly in the morning. You are the only man to whom I have ever told that secret."

The lawyer changed. He began to tell other men what had happened to him and how God had answered the defeats and compromises in his life. He got honest with his wife, and their home became new. The leaders of China heard the news and many others, like Sun Yat-sen, found their way to Frank Buchman's door as a result of what happened to men like the Chinese lawyer.

Bishop Lewis of China recorded that the work done by Buchman and his friends at that time in the Far East had meant more to Chinese leadership than any single movement during the twenty-eight years the Bishop had spent in China.

It was in those early years that Frank Buchman first began to understand the depth of degradation even in the lives of those who called themselves Christian. He began to tackle problems of perversion in the lives of many who had no hesitation in living in defeat, while preaching the Gospel of Christ. It was now that Buchman first felt the viciousness of opposition from men in the grip of such sins as homosexual indulgence who felt the edge of his challenge and refused to change.

In China, too, Buchman first met the opposition of Communists who understood that if God were restored to leadership throughout the world, there would be no chance of success for the revolution about which Lenin said, "It can never succeed until the myth of God is removed from the mind of man."

In India, too, in those years, miracles in men marked the friendships formed by Frank Buchman.

After meeting Gandhi in Madras in 1915, Buchman was invited by the headmaster of a famous public school to come to the school camp. The master complained about a boy called Victor. This boy was in rebellion. He used to pull out the tent pegs and let the tents fall on the people inside. He never would come to any of the camp meetings. The men in charge had decided that Victor must immediately be sent home.

Buchman said, "Have you talked to the boy?"

The master replied, "No, we have talked about him. But will you talk to him?"

Buchman agreed. And the master promised he would have

the boy to meet Frank Buchman at 10:30 in the morning. Victor did not turn up. At lunch the master asked how the talk had gone.

Buchman replied, "No Victor."

"Oh, but he promised," said the master.

"A lot of people say yes when they mean no," replied Buchman. "See if you can get him to meet me at 2:30."

So Buchman waited while most people were having an afternoon rest. Still there was no sign of Victor. At tea-time the master said, "But he promised me he would come to see you."

That night there was a beautiful full moon. Victor had promised to come to see Buchman but instead he was off in a boat rowing on the canal. "Who could blame Victor for staying away?" asked Buchman.

Next morning at 11 o'clock the master came running in saying, "I have got Victor, come at once." Buchman went out to a small hill where Victor and another boy were playing. They were playing with bamboo canes and twirling them like batons that are twirled by drum-majors at the head of marching bands.

Buchman went up to Victor and said, "You do that so well. I wish I could do it."

Victor, who had the habit of running away when any older person approached him, replied, "Well, try it."

Buchman tried it and failed. This failure delighted Victor. Then Buchman sat down and said to Victor, "I once went to camp. I hated it."

Victor said, "Were you like that? I am just like it too."

He then began to tell Buchman about how he was making a nuisance of himself everywhere and pulling up the tent pegs. He said, "There is something wrong inside me. That's all that can be said about it."

After further talk Victor said, "I am sorry."

"How much sorry?" said Buchman. "Do you know what remorse is?"

Victor said, "Yes, I know. It is being sorry and then going ahead and doing it again."

"That's not much good," said Buchman.

"No," replied Victor, "what I need is repentance. That means being sorry enough to quit."

Frank Buchman was so impressed by Victor's understanding of the difference between remorse and repentance that he used the boy's definitions for the rest of his life.

Then Buchman said to Victor, "You can have a friend who always understands you, always sticks with you and is so interesting you never want to run away from Him."

Victor said, "I know who you mean. You mean Jesus Christ. I'd like to be His friend, but I don't know how."

Buchman talked to the boy on that Himalayan hillside about sin with the big "I" as its middle letter. He said that sin is anything which comes between you and God or between you and the other fellow. He told him how he had gone on his knees and given all of himself that he knew to all that he knew of God.

Victor said, "I'd like to do that." He went on his knees with Buchman and said, "Lord, manage me, for I can't manage myself."

Later he said to Buchman, "It's as if a lot of old luggage had rolled away that was no good. I must go and tell my friends what has happened to me."

Buchman said to him, "If Jesus is your best friend, then it's plain bad manners not to introduce him to other people."

When the school went to the railway station to leave the camp, the master said to Buchman, "What in the world has happened to Victor? He is absolutely different."

Buchman said, "I think you'd better ask Victor."

But Victor was not there. He had seen a police guard with a prisoner handcuffed to him, being taken off to jail. He went up to the prisoner and said, "I'm sorry. I was like you until a few hours ago. I was a prisoner to all the things I did wrong. There was a man called Paul who was a prisoner. But even though he was in prison he was a free man, and you can be a free man too. I'll see you when you come out of prison and tell you more about it." Then Victor went and bought the handcuffed man some curry and rice.

Months later Frank Buchman visited Victor at his school and met many of his fellow students, Muslims and Hindus, as well as boys from Britain, who had been changed because of talking with Victor.

The story spread through India. Later a Bishop met Buchman and said to him, "I don't need any introduction to you. I've seen Victor." The Bishop then asked Frank Buchman to go to England and do the same thing for a relative of his at Cambridge University. It was this suggestion from the Bishop that sent Frank Buchman to Britain and began the work in Cambridge University and then in Oxford University that was the start of the spread of Moral Re-Armament throughout the world.

To the end of his life Buchman's secret of dealing with men remained the same as that which he used in dealing with Victor or the Chinese lawyer.

In 1959, Saburo Chiba, then Chairman of the Security

Committee of the Japanese Diet, came to spend one day with Buchman.

Some of the people staying with Buchman at that time said, "Chiba has had a long journey. He has come from Japan, all through Asia, all through Europe, all through America, and he will be tired. Give him a good room and let him rest." Buchman replied, "Here is a man who can affect the life of an entire nation. Rest? Let's use every minute of the day to give him a maximum experience of change."

Chiba arrived with his wife. He was an agnostic. He was friendly, but cautious. He sat down to breakfast with Buchman and his friends at a quarter-past eight in the morning. The breakfast lasted until twenty minutes to twelve. Stories were told of how racial differences in South Africa and the Southern States of America were being answered by a change in men. How Archbishop Makarios, the Greek, and Dr. Kutchuk, the Turk, both said Moral Re-Armament had played an important part in bringing the bloodshed on Cyprus to an end. How Communists in Germany, Italy, Kerala and every part of the world said that in Moral Re-Armament they found an idea superior to Communism because it created a new type of man and filled the deepest needs in the human heart.

After breakfast the men walked together in the garden and talked. Lunch was a Japanese meal, perfectly cooked. Chiba was so impressed he insisted on going into the kitchen to meet the cooks. He found there the daughter of a Wall Street banker who told him that she had given her life, without salary of any kind, to cook perfect meals for the guests who came to that home. Chiba said to Frank Buchman, "If you have an idea that turns a Wall Street banker's daughter into a cook, and a cook as perfect as that one, and she does that without being paid one cent, it's certainly a very big idea."

At the end of that afternoon, as Chiba and his wife were preparing to leave, Buchman said to him, "I had one thought early this morning for you."

Chiba said, "What was it?"

Buchman said, "The whole world will walk into your heart. You will let the whole world walk into your heart."

As Chiba, the agnostic statesman, said goodbye at the airport that evening, he turned to his friends with these words: "Today, for the first time in my life, I have found God. I shall never be the same again."

His whole family life, since that time, has been transformed. His grand-daughter, Emiko, is working with Moral Re-Armament. She changed and wrote a letter to every member of her family putting right things that had been wrong. This helped her mother to change and her father too. Emiko's younger sister was a brilliant girl, but with a heart that was somewhat cold. She changed and is a woman with a warmth that makes friends everywhere she goes. Chiba's son began to change. He walked up and down outside his father's room until two o'clock in the morning before he found the courage to go in and be honest with him.

Chiba said, "My son has found how to tell right from wrong; my grand-daughter has found direction for her life; and I myself have found the courage to say anything to anyone."

Chiba took a keen interest in helping to change the leaders of the Seinendan, the great Japanese youth organization with a membership of four-and-a-half million. Buchman heard that Moscow had invited over a hundred of the Seinendan to Russia for training. He cabled inviting them to come to a Moral Re-Armament assembly instead. There was strong discussion. In the end a hundred and two of the Seinendan leadership came to Moral Re-Armament for training and only seven went to Moscow.

For three months, night and day, Frank Buchman and his friends worked to bring moral change and a faith in God to the leadership of the Seinendan. Many of them were Marxist and anti-West. Buchman's friends had to deal with adultery, illegitimate children, homosexuality, self-abuse, lesbianism among women, incest, sterilization, dope-taking and dishonesty over money. At the end of the three months, all but a few of the young Japanese had been changed. They returned to their country and were so effective in their leadership that since that time every Communist candidate in the elections for the executive of the Seinendan has been defeated, and everyone elected has been someone trained by Moral Re-Armament. A Communist leader said to one of the successful candidates, "You beat us." The Moral Re-Armament man replied, "An idea beat you." The Communist said, "The people trained in Moral Re-Armament are incorruptible."

Nobosuke Kishi, as Prime Minister of Japan, telephoned to Frank Buchman from Blair House when he was in Washington as President Eisenhower's guest. He asked what Buchman was doing for the leadership of the Japanese youth. Buchman replied, "We are teaching them to go not Left, not Right, but Straight." On his return to his country, Kishi told the Press he wanted to lead Japan not Left, not Right, but Straight. Later at a press conference he gave his opinion that Japan would have gone behind the Bamboo Curtain in

1960 were it not for the men and women, in every walk of life, changed and trained in Moral Re-Armament.

The crisis of 1960, to which Mr. Kishi referred, was brought about by the students of Tokyo, led by the Zengakuren organization. They rioted in the streets of Tokyo and prevented President Eisenhower, as he then was, from visiting Japan. A number of the Zengakuren students were invited to Europe for training in Moral Re-Armament. They came. They changed. Some were honest about how they had accepted money from the Communist Party to create the disturbances in Tokyo. They wrote a play called *The Tiger*, which shows with passion and reality how, through moral compromise, men can be taken over to play their part in corrupting and communizing their country. This play went to Germany and to France and then to the United States. There, James Hagerty, who had been Eisenhower's press secretary for many years, saw it. Hagerty had gone to Tokyo to prepare the path for Eisenhower. He had been mobbed at the airport, and Eisenhower's visit was cancelled.

At the end of the play in America, Hagerty met the Zengakuren students. One of them said to him, "I was at the airport in Tokyo by the side of your car."

Hagerty replied, "I remember you well. You not only stood beside my car, but you climbed onto the roof and beat on it with your fists." Hagerty told the students that what he had seen on the stage was the greatest demonstration of change and of an ideology superior to the materialism of East and West that he had ever seen. He told the students, "You don't need to apologize to me. What I saw on that stage tonight is the best apology that could be given to a man or nation."

From Hagerty they went to Eisenhower. They spoke in such terms to Eisenhower that he told them, "I am with you a hundred per cent. I want you to go to Latin America and give your message there."

The Zengakuren students went to Brazil, Peru and other Latin American countries with their play. In five months over one million people in theatres and vast stadiums saw their play and heard their challenge. More than twenty million others saw and heard it over the television. At times seventy million a day had the news of their advance through the radio and through the columns of the Chateaubriand press and other newspapers.

When the President of Brazil heard of what they were doing, he ordered the Air Force, Army and Navy to transport them, a force of more than 200 people, wherever they wanted to go. They travelled 15,000 miles over vast tracts of country and spoke in areas so full of poverty and bitterness that tanks had been out to control rioting crowds only a week or two before.

When the President of Brazil resigned and there was a threat of armed uprising in the country, Eudocio Ravines, the man who had been commissioned by Moscow to inaugurate the Communist Party in Peru and other parts of Latin America, said, "That force, with the play *The Tiger*, has saved the whole of Brazil from civil war."

FOUR

"*Fire from Heaven*"

When Frank Buchman first went to Latin America in 1931, his host was his old friend the Chinese lawyer who was now Chinese Minister in Chile.

This man gave an official dinner for Buchman. At it, he stood up and told the diplomats and leaders of the country how he had been changed. He had been made Governor of his native city in China. A Soviet agent came to the place with the task of bringing Communism to the whole province. The Communist told this Chinese diplomat that he would have to give up the message he was now bringing to his people or riots would be organized and his head would be cut off and carried on a pole through the streets of his native city. The Chinese diplomat told the Communist that he might cut off his head, but he would not be able to make him trim his convictions. He said to the Communist, "Jesus Christ is my personal friend and I will never betray Him."

Buchman went to Peru. Sir Charles Bentinck was British

Ambassador there at that time. He had become a friend of Buchman's when he saw the change in the family of his Dutch relatives, the van Heeckerens of Rhederoord. The van Heeckerens are still working at the heart of Moral Re-Armament.

It was in Lima that Sir Charles introduced Buchman to a Peruvian taxi driver. This driver took a liking to Frank Buchman. He became his personal chauffeur throughout his stay in Lima. Frank Buchman used to go and visit the chauffeur in his home. He met his family. The chauffeur said it was the first time anybody he had been employed to drive in a car had taken the trouble to visit his home. The family changed.

The men and women of Peru are passionate and many of them are poor. Another revolution broke out. At this time the Prince of Wales, as he then was, was visiting the city. Those responsible for his welfare were afraid. The Prince could not move from the place he was staying. The streets were barricaded. There was rifle-fire all over the city. Men were being killed.

The Hungarian, Bela Kun, was also there. He was staying in the same hotel as the Prince of Wales and Frank Buchman. His task was to organize Communist revolution in Peru and throughout the continent.

In the midst of the upheaval and danger, the chauffeur arrived at the hotel with his car. He said to Frank Buchman, "You may not know it, but I am a friend of the men who are leading this revolution. I know their plans. I know what they are going to do. I can go anywhere I like in the city. So if you want to drive around today, don't let the rifle-fire or the barricades stop you."

Buchman at once accepted this offer. Throughout the

revolution he and those with him moved freely about in the chauffeur's car.

These events, and the lessons he learned in the revolutionary situation in Latin America, made a mark on the thinking of Frank Buchman for the rest of his life. Later in 1931 he was talking to the students in Aberdeen University. He told them of the revolutionary situation in Latin America. He said, "As I watched the flames of a burning city making the night sky red, guidance came to me as if written in letters of fire. It was: 'We need emboldened leadership to meet the present world crisis.'"

Then Frank Buchman told those Aberdeen students that every member of the Government in the country in Latin America from which he had just come, had two young Communist agents attached to him to ensure that he followed the Communist Party line. It was at a time in modern history when Communism meant little to the ordinary man or statesman. People thought of Communists as odd individuals with beards and bombs. They did not wholly like them, but did not take them seriously.

Buchman took them very seriously indeed. His experiences in China, Latin America and throughout the world led him to the belief that man was faced with an intelligent, ruthless, ceaseless attempt by some of the cleverest men in the world to alter the nature of civilization and to win every continent to a godless ideology. He challenged the students of Aberdeen, "Where among you are the men who will lay down your lives to attach yourselves to governments in the future and bring the answer to them, just as these Communists have attached themselves to the men running the Latin American countries today?"

One of the students who accepted the challenge came

and spoke to Frank Buchman about it. Buchman made it plain that the student would never do the job unless his own life was straight and clean. The student said to Buchman, "I want to be one of the men who will bring this answer to the world. I want to give my life to the work you are doing." This statement was made on the platform of a Scottish station, just before the night train for London left. Buchman took the young man into the train and said, "Let us have guidance together." Buchman's guidance for him was, "You are ambitious. You want to do this for your own sake, not for the sake of Christ. 'Young man, seekest thou great things for thyself? Seek them not. Seek Christ.'"

That man accepted the challenge and the lesson. He has worked at Buchman's side in many countries and for thirty years. Until the end of his life Buchman still continued to fight for his development as a man of God. But he had a sense of humor in the way he did it. When this man drove some friends of Buchman through a night from the South of England to Scotland, he was determined to drive on to the other side of Scotland. He was too tired to drive in safety but too wilful to stop. Buchman urged him to stay and sleep. The man persisted. Finally Buchman took him down the corridor to the door of the room that had been set aside for him. He pointed to a card with the man's name written on it. He said with a laugh, "You can't waste all that ink!" So the man laughed too—and stayed. He says that he found in his friendship with Buchman the answer to the steel of the pride that governed him.

This man, with others, has played a part in welcoming and training the hundreds of men and women from Brazil and Latin America who, in 1961, have journeyed to Europe for training in Moral Re-Armament. They came as the result of decisions taken in the lives of men like General Bethlem. Here is the way Frank Buchman told some of the story in his own words in a speech called *Solid Rock or Sinking Sand*, given through the press and radio to millions of people throughout the world just three months before he died:

"A month ago I sent an Easter message to the world, *All the Moral Fences Are Down*. There was an instant response. From the statesmen and the ordinary man, in country after country, came the word, 'That is the problem. Help us to rebuild those moral fences for our nations and the world.'

"General Bethlem of Brazil is a man who is doing just that. In Miami, Florida, he dropped down on a group of leaders from all the hemisphere. There was the General commanding the army of Peru. There was the President of the Parliament from Uruguay. There was the representative of the Minister of War from Argentina, the wife of the Minister of Reconstruction of Chile, dockers' leaders and industrialists from Brazil. There was the man who founded the Communist Party in Peru and brought in the first Popular Front Government in Chile.

"There General Bethlem also met General Inoue from Japan, and with him the force of Japanese youth with *The Tiger*, their play about the answer to the Tokyo riots. He met Chief Walking Buffalo from Canada with his Braves and Counsellors. He met businessmen from Switzerland, labor leaders from France and Germany. He met Philip Vundla, elected spokesman for 600,000 Africans, whom the police once described as the most dangerous man in South Africa; and Vaitheswaran, six years a dedicated Communist in South India, whose change has helped give Kerala the solid rock of an answer to Communism. He met William Pawley, son of a former United States Ambassador to Peru and Brazil. From Britain he met Peter Howard, the author, and Rear-Admiral Sir Edward Cochrane, great-nephew of the famous Lord Cochrane who helped liberate Chile, Peru and Brazil. He met a Jamaican leader who said, 'You men have the only hope for the Caribbean. We must mobilize now for this answer, otherwise we shall quickly go the way of Cuba.'

"General Bethlem had held two diplomatic posts as Ambassador of Brazil to Bolivia and Pakistan, but now he was on a trip with his wife for a holiday in New York. As he listened to these men speak, he was gripped by their unity that was like a rock because God was in command. This was the answer for the hemisphere. Within a week he had turned around and was leading an advance force of these very men to Brazil, which was followed a few days later by a planeload of 129 from twenty-four countries, to initiate what the newspaper *El País* of Montevideo called, 'The greatest ideological offensive undertaken on the Latin American continent.' The General eagerly went back to give Brazil the solid foundation for world leadership that he had longed for for his nation. As his advance-guard he took with him Rajmohan Gandhi of India, Admiral Cochrane, Vaitheswaran, and Takasumi Mitsui of the great Japanese industrial family. They prepared the way.

"When the main international force arrived they were met by radio, press and television. In fact, one enthusiastic television cameraman got on the plane before the visitors could get off. It was national news.

"Immediately they spoke at a lunch to four hundred leading industrialists and businessmen, including the representatives of Ford, General Electric, Goodyear Rubber and Swifts. General Bethlem said, 'Both North and South America are at the most critical points of our history. Against the background of Cuba, Venezuela and Bolivia where I have been Ambassador, and the new Russian offensive starting in Mexico on May Day, the inescapable choice for Latin America is Moral Re-Armament or Communism.

"'I know you businessmen, because I was like you. We ask our wives to live purity, but we are not pure. We ask our workers to be honest, but we are dishonest. I have changed and committed my whole life to this fight.'

"To General Bethlem's surprise and astonishment these businessmen three times halted his presentation at that lunch with standing ovations. Some people may say this is an incredible response, but here is the fact. Immediately General Bethlem and his force were invited to speak to a meeting of six hundred leaders of the industrial and business life of Brazil and to take an hour-and-a-half's television program.

"Chief Walking Buffalo of the Stoney Indians and his party created such a stir coming to this luncheon that hundreds of school children crowded into the lobby to meet him. He spoke of the time he made me a blood-brother twenty-eight years ago, when he gave me the name of *A Wo Zan Zan Tonga*—Great Light in Darkness. While the Chief was speaking, there came a message from across the street from the Mother Superior of São Paulo's most famous convent school for seven hundred children from leading families, asking him to come with his friends to speak to a quickly convened school assembly. The response was electric. Said the Mother Superior, 'This will be a marking day in the annals of this college.' Said another Sister, 'This is the work of the Holy Spirit.'

"This can be the normal life of these countries, for which people have been saying there is not much hope. Otherwise these businessmen and their families with all their money and social life will lead to an absence of God, spelling the breakdown of the moral fences of democracy, and eventually to Communism.

"On May Day the Japanese launched their ideological weapon *The Tiger* in Latin America. Crowds outside the Municipal Theatre in São Paulo were so great that the traffic was stopped. Former Prime Minister Kishi of Japan cabled: 'Tonight is being followed by millions of Japanese who are joining this fight to root out Communism, exploitation and slavery all around the world.'"

In a few months General Bethlem has begun to affect the history of his own country and his own continent. It came through simple moral decisions. He saw a play called *The Ladder*. Bethlem said, "On the stage that night, I saw the picture of myself, using every situation and every friendship to climb higher up the ladder of life. I decided to give my life to bring an answer."

He and his wife were at that time on their way to New York for a shopping holiday. They cancelled their plans. They gave their money, saved for the shopping expedition, to the work of Moral Re-Armament.

They went back home. General Bethlem immediately closed his office and ended all professional activities. He was determined to yield every secondary aim and to go all out to answer the division and corruption in the masses and the leadership of his country.

In June 1961, General Bethlem brought 115 of his countrymen and others from Latin America by special plane to Caux to meet Frank Buchman. Among them was Marshal Juarez Tavora, national hero of Brazil, who has played a part in every revolution in the last forty years there. He calls MRA

"The final revolution to put right what is wrong throughout the entire world."

When the time came to return to South America, these men came to take leave of Frank Buchman. With all the force at his command he said to them, "Millions, millions, millions will see in you the hope of a new world order." Then he added, "God will hold you fast–if you will let Him."

Tavora and Bethlem led the MRA force of people from twenty-eight nations through the Communist-dominated riot center of North-East Brazil. Tens of thousands poured into stadiums to see *The Tiger*. The Archbishop of Natal, one of eight Archbishops who received them, said, "Moral Re-Armament is fire from Heaven to purify the earth. It is a mighty army of the heart, intellect and will. It is arming and preparing the world of tomorrow."

A thousand miles up the Amazon in Manaus, ninety thousand people flooded the football stadium for the MRA play on Cuba's National Day, while only forty people turned out for the Castro demonstration in the nearby public square.

From Manaus the Brazilian Air Force which, with the Navy and the Army, had carried the force through the country, shuttled them another thousand miles across the Amazon jungle into Iquitos, Peru, where President Prado had invited them to do for Peru what had already been done in Brazil.

In Lima, when they heard that Frank Buchman had died in Freudenstadt, sixty thousand Peruvians in the National Stadium stood there in silent tribute to him.

FIVE

Africa with an Answer

A few weeks before he died, two of Frank Buchman's friends stood together and spoke on a public platform.

One man was black, the other white. One was Philip Q. Vundla, elected spokesman for 600,000 Africans in the Johannesburg area, and for many years one of the militant leaders of the African people in South Africa.

The other was John Trengove, Queen's Counsel, one of the Government prosecutors in the South African Treason Trials which lasted over three years and had been used by many people to sow seeds of hate and bitterness in nations around the earth.

These two men spoke unitedly of how through change they had found an unshakable unity. A reporter of international experience said: "Although I saw this happen with my own eyes I still find it hard to believe."

Trengove said: "Philip Vundla's speeches were some of the most potent evidence in the trials. Here at Caux I have listened to Mr. Vundla and have seen the passion and fire of the answer to hatred and bitterness he has found. I am coming to realize how my way of living—and the living of white men like me—has fed the hatred and bitterness of men like Vundla."

After describing how 6000 Africans organized by the African National Congress, of which Vundla was a part, had defied the laws in Port Elizabeth in 1952, Trengove continued: "They were men of courage and determination but they were filled with bitterness and hatred against the white man. We became more superior, selfish and soft—they became more bitter and full of hatred. The result was bursts of violence, boycotts, destruction and outbreaks such as Sharpeville."

"Through my friendship with Frank Buchman and with men like Philip Vundla, I have come to accept the Cross, to give up what is wrong and to take on what is right, to face my motives and to see that I have always wanted to make people understand my country, instead of accepting the cost of my sin and the cost of my nation's sins. Unless we, from end to end of Africa, learn to live like sons of God, we will never find lasting peace."

Vundla, the African revolutionary, said, "For the love of God, let us become real men and fight for what is right together. Many African leaders say, 'We can use Communism to cross a river. But when we are the other side of the river we will abandon Communism.' But experience shows that by the time we reach the other bank we are the prisoners of the force we tried to use. I will stand with any man of any color who lays aside all concern for reputation and position and gives everything to bring Moral Re-Armament to Africa and the world.

"South Africa is being used all over the world to divide men on the issues of black and white. I know personally African leaders who have been trained in Peking and Moscow. The situation in my country is so explosive that it could come to a blood-bath."

Vundla described how six men burst into his house, stabbed him in the back and left him for dead because he was challenging black as well as white to change. He said that no violence could stop him and countless Africans like himself who saw, through change in men like Trengove and others, the first hope for generations of an Africa free from hate, fear and greed, and peopled by free men and women.

Frank Buchman began his work in South Africa in 1928. He was in Florence. Queen Sophie of Greece heard he planned to visit South Africa. She gave him letters to the Governor-General, the Earl of Athlone, great-uncle to the present Queen of England.

In South Africa Buchman presented his letters. He talked with the Governor-General for an hour. Then Athlone took him out to the motor car that was waiting. But as the door of the car was opened, Athlone said, "We have not talked about the thing that interests me most. What I really want to know is how you get hold of a man like George Daneel and change him. You've not told me. Come on inside again." So the two men turned and went back indoors.

George Daneel was a Springbok. This is the name given to men who play rugby football for South Africa. They are national heroes.

Daneel comes from the heart of Afrikanerdom. His background and straightforwardness are such that cabinet ministers heed him. He came to take morning tea with Frank

Buchman. He said to him, "People around you seem to change."

Buchman replied, "Of course. Don't they change when they are around you?"

Daneel had to say that they did not. Buchman said, "Why is that?"

Daneel decided that he would stay to lunch and talk more with Frank Buchman. Then he stayed to tea. Then he stayed to dinner. Then he stayed for life.

He found an answer that day to habits of impurity which had robbed him of the power to change people.

One man he changed is Dr. William Nkomo, founder and first President of the African National Congress Youth League. This League was one of the most revolutionary movements in South Africa. Nkomo describes its aims by saying, "I believed that the hope for the African lay only in a bloodbath where every white man would be slain or driven into the sea."

Nkomo, in 1953, heard Daneel speak at an assembly at Lusaka, in Northern Rhodesia. Nkomo said, "I saw white men change and black men change, and I myself changed."

The Afrikaners called Nkomo a Communist. He called them Fascists. He now says, "I have always been a revolutionary. In Moral Re-Armament I saw something greater than nationalism at work. I saw an ideology superior to all other ideologies because it is for everyone everywhere. This is the road which will be best for my people and for South Africa."

On September 10, 1961, Nkomo spoke with Trengove at a public meeting in Newclare, the district of Johannesburg where gang warfare used to break out week by week. Leading Communists have their homes there. These two men spoke to an audience which included people who had travelled over forty miles from Sharpeville, the scene of the shooting tragedy in 1960.

The Earl of Athlone kept his friendship with Daneel and his interest in the work these men were doing, until the end of his life. These white and black South Africans were entertained at his home in Kensington Palace, and members of the British Cabinet were invited there to hear what they had to say. He was interested in the judgment of the Hon. J. H. Hofmeyr who, as Deputy Prime Minister of South Africa, cabled to the British House of Commons: "Dr. Buchman's visit to South Africa in 1929 was of national significance. It started a major and continuing influence for racial reconciliation throughout the whole country, white and black, Dutch and British. The future of democratic institutions in South Africa may well depend largely on the fruits of their labors."

Athlone broadcast to the whole British Commonwealth during the war, saying: "The call for Moral Re-Armament has encircled the world and become a source of fresh hope to millions of men and women. It calls on us to make the Will of God the guiding force, as for individuals, so for homes and nations."

Buchman's dealings with people were not always long in time, but almost always so penetrating and accurate that the effect lasted. At the time when the Congo was about to become free, some Congolese and Belgians came to talk with him.

A Belgian said to Buchman, "We are lucky in the Congo. We have no real hatred there."

There was silence. Then one of the Congolese said, "You are mistaken. There is hatred in the Congo."

The Belgian smiled and said, "I know the country pretty well. You can take it from me that though we may have a difference here and there, your people and mine do not hate each other."

The Congolese said, "There is a black list of the Belgians whom my friends and I mean to kill when we get our freedom. I know of the list because I helped to draw it up. Until I met Frank Buchman and his friends, I would have been one of those who took part in the killings. If that is not hate, what is it?"

Then another Belgian spoke out boldly: "What you say is true. There is hatred, and men like myself have caused it. I was a Governor in the Congo for over twenty years. I lived on the fat of the land and treated men like you as inferiors. I have seen here the wrongfulness of it. Mine is the selfishness that threatens to destroy freedom and decency throughout the world. I am deeply sorry and I hope you will be able to forgive me."

Buchman suggested that everybody should be quiet and listen to the voice of God speaking in their hearts. The men left that room changed and reconciled. They went back to the Congo together. The list of Belgians due to be slain was destroyed. In spite of the terrible events that have since taken place in that part of Africa, there are men walking the earth today who would be under it, but for that time spent in Frank Buchman's room.

In September 1961, Madame Joseph Kasavubu, wife of the President of the Congo, led a delegation to the Assembly for Moral Re-Armament at Caux. She spoke on behalf of all the Congolese delegates who had come for training in Moral Re-Armament through the months beforehand. She said, "We put all our trust in you. You will help us free the Congo from its difficulties. The work Dr. Buchman has built will continue to sweep forward throughout the world."

Adolphe Kasavubu, eldest son of the President, said, "Here is the place where unity can be found. If enough of my countrymen come to Caux and learn the truth of Moral Re-Armament, the Congo will come forth from her difficulties."

Kasavubu reported that the leaders of the Baluba and Lulua tribes had been reconciled before a meeting of 5000 people in Leopoldville, at which his father, the President, and members of his cabinet were present. Grand Chief Kalamba of the Lulua said there, "I promised Frank Buchman I would do this, and I have kept my word." Kasavubu said that, even two months before, people in the Congo would have thought it impossible to make peace between tribes which for generations had been savage enemies. He said, "We are in the midst of a battle. This reconciliation is a first step and a big step. We must continue the fight. Congo is at the heart of Africa. If Congo goes Communist, all Africa will follow. People give money to the countries they call under-developed. That is not enough. You must win and change the hearts of men. An ideology is needed: otherwise dollars will not count. That ideology is Moral Re-Armament."

After speaking of the 483 MRA broadcasts given in the previous twelve months over Leopoldville radio, Cyrille Nzao, *Chef de Cabinet* of President Kasavubu, said, "My deepest longing is that Moral Re-Armament shall permeate the whole world. Here is the answer to the tidal wave of Communism, and also to the imperialism that is being swept out of Africa. We are determined to strengthen and live Moral Re-Armament, so as to set all the nations free, and keep them free."

It was Robert Schuman, former Prime Minister of France, who sent Frank Buchman to North Africa. Schuman came to Caux. At the end of a morning assembly there, he asked to speak. He said, "I go to conference after conference. Normally they end in great disappointment. Here I find nothing but a great hope."

Then he went across and, in Gallic style, embraced Buchman on both cheeks. At lunch the two friends talked of North Africa. Morocco was in turmoil. Schuman said, "You must go there."

Buchman answered, "Morocco? That's not the place for me. I don't speak any Arabic and, although I spent some time trying to learn French at Grenoble as a young man, the only French I can remember is *mauvais garçon!*"

Schuman laughed. He said, "*Mauvais garçon* is enough to take you most places in the world, including Morocco or France."

Buchman went to Morocco. He took a few friends with him. French settlers changed. At first the Moroccan nationalists believed it was an imperialist trick. Then one of their leaders heard of a Frenchman who had called his workers together and said to them, "I have a cellar of wine. For me it is an indulgence. To you, as Moslems, it is an offense. It is time that Frenchmen like myself ended the indulgences that offend men like you. Will you help me to destroy my cellar of wine?"

The Moroccan workers carried the Frenchman's bottles outside the house and broke them so that the wine soaked into the dust and the hard, sun-baked earth. They did it rejoicing. When the nationalist leader heard this true tale, he said, "Such a Frenchman is not bluffing. This is real."

The nationalist leader was determined to meet Buchman.

He came to Caux and changed. Someone said to him, "You are as near to God as you are to the person from whom you are most divided." His bitterest enemy was El Glaoui, the Pasha of Marrakesh, whose actions had led to the exile of the Sultan by the French. The nationalist apologized to El Glaoui for his hatred. The Pasha was moved to tears. Within a week the impossible happened. El Glaoui prostrated himself before the Sultan and asked his forgiveness. *The Times* of London wrote: "Today's meeting seems to mark the final reconciliation between these two adversaries. And El Glaoui's gesture, for all its apparent abasement, has nobility and grandeur."

Shortly afterward the Sultan was able to return to his country. He became King Mohammed V. Later France gave Morocco her liberty and the land was saved from bloodshed.

His Sheriffian Majesty the King sent this message to Buchman: "I thank you for all you have done for Morocco, the Moroccans and myself in these testing years. Moral Re-Armament must become for us Moslems just as much an incentive as it is for you Christians and for all nations. Material re-armament alone has been proved a failure. Moral Re-Armament remains the essential. My desire is that your message, which is founded on the essential moral values and the Will of God, reaches the masses of this country. We have complete confidence in the work you are doing."

The change in men which began when Buchman visited Morocco, spread to Tunisia. Speaking in Washington in June 1955, Mohammed Masmoudi, Minister of State and one of the leaders of the new Tunisia, said, "Were it not for MRA, Tunisia today would be engaged in a war without mercy against the French. Moral Re-Armament is bridging the gap between France and Tunisia, between Africa and Europe. Africa is awakening. She is determined to play her part in world affairs within the framework of MRA. Without MRA Tunisia would have been another Indo-China."

President Bourguiba said later, "The world must be told of the effect of Moral Re-Armament in my country." And Robert Schuman said, "Without Moral Re-Armament the history of Morocco and Tunisia would be far different."

From end to end of Africa, men whose lives were changed as a result of meeting Buchman and talking with him, are spreading his secret of changing other men.

At a time when Africa is calling on the white man to leave, leaders of seventeen countries of Africa urged Frank Buchman to come, and bring with him the men and women of Moral Re-Armament.

An African leader summed up Buchman's work in these words: "Moral Re-Armament is doing for Africa what Abraham Lincoln did for America. It is binding up the nations' wounds and setting the people free."

SIX

Who Changes Hate, Changes History

Late one night in the year 1960, the telephone bell in Frank Buchman's home in America rang. It was a newspaperman of United Press International asking for his comments on a statement made that afternoon at a press conference in Atlanta, Georgia. A leading German diplomat was visiting America. The reporters had asked him, "What is the most significant political development in Europe since World War II?" His reply was, "The new accord and understanding between Germany and France, which I believe is permanent. For this the work of Moral Re-Armament is largely responsible."

A year or two before this, Chancellor Adenauer of Germany had told the press that Moral Re-Armament has played "an unseen but effective part in important international agreements."

Frank Buchman's work with people, man by man, country by country, is the seed from which this crop has been reaped.

One man whom Buchman helped is called Max Bladeck. He is a coal miner from the Ruhr. He was head of the works council of one of the largest collieries there. He was twenty-five years a member of the Communist Party. He was a militant atheist.

Just after the war Buchman's friends were holding hundreds of meetings in factories and trade union branches in the Ruhr as well as in the Provincial Parliaments of Western Germany. They were living in the homes of the miners for months. Bladeck did his best to destroy them. In the end he came with other Communist friends to Caux. There he was challenged as a revolutionary to make an experiment in absolute moral standards of honesty, purity, unselfishness and love, applied to his own life. He began to change. On their return to the Ruhr, Bladeck and these other Communist leaders were called before the Communist Party Executive. They said, "We have found in Moral Re-Armament an ideology greater than Communism."

The West German Communist Party was in a difficulty. For years Leninist strategy had been for Communism to infiltrate into the structure of society and change it. Here were men from the hard core of the party who went to Caux and themselves began to change. Finally, the West German Communist Party had to remove forty regional leaders of the Party for having "dealings with a contrary ideology."

The explanation given by the West German Communist Party was, "Moral Re-Armament aims at the re-education of man and the reconciliation of classes and therefore confuses fighters for class war."

Bladeck became known in the Ruhr as a Moral Re-Armament man. The Communist Party made every effort to win him back. They knew one weakness in his life was drink. They managed to get him drinking and put him in touch with a woman. Bladeck fell into compromise in his cups. At once, all over the Ruhr, the Communists began to point him out and say, "That is how men from Caux live. It is hypocrisy." Bladeck was so shaken and ashamed that he wrote Frank Buchman asking that no more of Buchman's friends should come to his home and that he should no longer be thought of as a friend of Buchman's or an ally of Moral Re-Armament. He said he had betrayed the cause in which he had believed.

Buchman was in America when he received Bladeck's letter. He cabled him back the following reply:

"Man-like it is to fall in sin;
Fiend-like it is to dwell therein;
Christ-like it is from sin to rise.

"The blood of Jesus Christ His Son cleanseth us from all sin. The biggest sinner can become the greatest saint. I have faith in the new Max. Sincerely, Frank."

Until that point, Bladeck had experienced something of moral change, but faith in God had been unreal to him. That cable shattered a core of atheism and cynicism within him. Faith was born. In the next few years hundreds of Marxists and Communists were changed. Many without faith found it.

When Bladeck was in India, news came that his father and mother had died within a few days of each other. After talking with his friend Frank Buchman, Bladeck asked more than two hundred people from countries in every part of the world to Catholic Mass in the Cathedral in memory of the faith of his family, and to honor the belief in God which he had found again.

Here in his own words is the story of how he was captured:

"When I gave my life to Communism, I believed it would give the world the right social order. Its means to that end is class struggle. Today I realize we simply divided humanity into two camps that hate and fight each other. In the atomic age, a class-conscious ideology like Communism is too small and has been superseded. Today I fight with Moral Re-Armament because it is not against Communism nor against capitalism: it goes to the root of evil and changes man, who is the cause of the failure of any system.

"I realized there was a tremendous difference between theory and practice. I used to speak at big meetings about equality, peace and freedom, but all the time at home there was no equality with my wife, nor peace with my neighbors—and no freedom in myself either, because I was a slave to nicotine and alcohol. I went to many meetings, but my wife did not know that some 'meetings' were not meetings. Everywhere I used to shout, 'Workers of the world, unite!' But at the same time I was dividing labor by my struggle for power.

"I saw that if I wanted to have a part in creating a new world order, I had to start with myself. That meant a revolutionary transformation of my living and thinking. I had to put things right in my family, in the mine and with all those who had been affected by my wrong motives. Through this experiment I saw very quickly that this ideology was based on a solid foundation, because if I can change, then this can be a reality for everyone in the world."

Germans like Bladeck learned to work shoulder to shoulder with leaders from France. One of these French was Irène Laure. She was for many years a leading figure of the French Socialist movement, member of the Executive of the Socialist Party, Member of Parliament for Marseilles, and a leader of the Socialist women of her country. She is a nurse by profession. She was a key figure in the Resistance movement in Southern France during the war. The Gestapo took her son and tortured him. She came out of the war dominated by her hatred of Germany. "I had only one wish," she says, "and that was to destroy them all."

She was invited to Caux and went, hoping to have a pleasant holiday with her family. On her first day there she heard Germans speaking to the assembly. She went straight back to her room and began to pack her bags. She said she would not stay in the same place as the Germans.

Coming out of her room she met Buchman who said to her, "You are a great fighter for the workers. You talk of uniting Europe. What sort of unity do you want in Europe if this is your attitude to the Germans?"

Irène Laure says of the days which followed, "They were days of inner turmoil. I wanted to find some 'flea in the straw' at Caux. But the moment came when I saw that hate can never create unity and that class war makes nonsense of the brotherhood of man.

"I needed a miracle to uproot hate from my heart. I hardly believed in God, but He performed that miracle. I became free to fight for the whole world, with one great desire—to restore for the past. I apologized to the Germans for having desired the total destruction of their country.

"I went with my husband and my son to Germany. There we spoke to ten out of the eleven West German parliaments. By the airlift we went to Berlin. We spoke on the radio, and at hundreds of meetings and interviews. We said we were sorry for the hate which had blinded us. We spoke of the answer to bitterness and of the possibility of building, through change in people, a hate-free world.

"Marxism is out of date in our age. For my husband, a militant Marxist for forty-six years and a pupil of the veteran Communist, Marcel Cachin, and for myself, it was not easy to face the fact that we had been wrong. But we saw that you can never build a new world, a united world, on hatred, jealousy and revenge, or by excluding one class or nation.

"Today France and Germany have found each other. A common ideology did for our countries what sentimentality never did between the wars."

The Laures went from end to end of Germany. She says of that time, "Can you think what it meant for me to go there? In my heart I had willed the ruins of World War II. I am a mother and grandmother. I am a Socialist and all my life I have talked about fraternity, yet I had longed for a whole people to be destroyed. I had to ask forgiveness for my hatred from those people who were living in the ruins. I had to ask forgiveness from 50,000 women whom I saw, grey with fatigue, clearing the rubble in Berlin. I do not forget the ruins in my own, or other countries, that the Germans caused. Not at all. But the thing I had to do was to face my own hatred and the part it played in dividing Europe, and to ask forgiveness for it.

"Change in me brought forth change in many Germans.

An idea strong enough to answer the hate I had, is strong enough to change the course of history."

Chancellor Adenauer said that Victor and Irène Laure did more than any other two people to build unity between the age-old enemies, Germany and France, in the last fifteen years. In 1960, he said of Frank Buchman's work, "Unless this work is carried forward, peace in the world cannot be maintained. A nation without an ideology is self-satisfied and dead. Communism is a false ideology, but it is an ideology, and can only be met with moral and spiritual weapons. We are in an ideological battle, and therein lies the decisive task. It may last decades, but it must be won. Now is the time to work more strongly than ever for unity through Moral Re-Armament. The one real hope of the nations living together in peace, is a change in the human heart."

When he met Frank Buchman in Los Angeles in March 1960, the German Chancellor said to him, "I must tell you how much I value you and your work of Moral Re-Armament. It is absolutely essential for the peace of the world."

In Italy, Don Luigi Sturzo, the patriot priest whose thinking inspired the Christian Democrat parties of Italy, France and Germany, described Buchman's work as "Fire from Heaven." He had heard of the miracles in men in families like the Biotello family. Their story is the story of so many of the workers of Europe and can be summed up in the words "poverty, unemployment, war and hate."

The father of the family lost both his feet in a tramway accident in Milan. He could never work again. The mother had to work at a factory bench, keeping her husband and five children alive. She did it for thirty years. She turned to Communism as the one hope, the idea to destroy a system that had made her suffer so greatly. The whole family was swept into the Communist Party. Her son, Remo, hated the Church. Then in 1954 her daughter, Rolanda, a Communist cell leader, met Buchman. Her whole life was changed. She decided to fight for the Moral Re-Armament of Italy. Her brother, Remo, bitterly opposed her. He called her a traitor to the working-class. But he could not deny that something had come into her life which freed her from bitterness and gave her the art of creating unity where division had been before.

Two years later Rolanda persuaded Remo to go to a play called *The Vanishing Island* which was being shown in Sesto san Giovanni, the "Little Stalingrad" of Italy and the fortress of Communism in the industrial North. The police estimated that more than 80 per cent of the audiences were Communist. The doors had to be barricaded to control the crowds. In one week 23,000 workers saw the play. Something shifted in Remo's heart. He said to his sister Rolanda, "You are right. I have been wrong. I have been trying to build a world free from hate when my own heart was full of hate. I must change. I see that it is reactionary to want the world different, but refuse to be different myself."

When Rolanda asked Remo where he felt he should begin, he said, "I who have talked so much about peace, must make peace with the family." He made apologies to his brother and his sister-in-law, and this action restored unity to a home which had been on the point of breaking.

Remo Biotello fell ill. He was taken to the Tramway Workers' Hospital in Milan, for he was Secretary-Treasurer of the Tramway Workers' Union, known as one of the most militant trade union bodies in Europe. It has 12,000 members and Remo Biotello was one of those who shaped their policy.

In hospital a tumor in his lung was discovered and surgery could not help it. Remo was in constant pain, but fought fearlessly and ceaselessly for change in doctors and patients alike. When they could do no more for him in hospital, he was sent home. He became too weak to write. But he had learned the secret of listening to God, having found faith again, and he used to dictate the thoughts that came to him to his sister Rolanda.

One day he told Marisa, his wife, "I must return to the Church. I want our marriage blessed by the Church. We must be married by a priest." Remo asked Marisa's foster-mother, called La Zia (Aunt), to go to the church and fetch the priest. La Zia had been a Communist for fifteen years. She, with Rolanda, had helped collect a million signatures for a Communist campaign. At first she refused to go and fetch the priest. But Remo, with his passion and his weakness, made her feel a compulsion to go. The priest was astounded when he saw her in church. He said, "Is the Devil coming to fetch Holy water?" La Zia was angry and left the church without a word. Remo, when he heard what happened, sent her back again. In the end the priest came to Remo's home. Remo and Marisa were married and blessed at Remo's bedside as he was by now too weak to move.

Then Remo heard the news that Buchman was coming through Milan on his way back to Caux from a journey in Asia. The thought came clearly to him: "Get up. Meet Frank Buchman. Tell him your convictions about this fight to change the world." His family thought he was mad to try to go to the station, but he said, "God told me to do it, and I will."

Buchman was only eleven minutes in Milan station. As he stepped off the train he said to Rolanda, there to greet him,

"How is Remo? I heard he was ill." Rolanda said, "Here he is to welcome you." Between those two men there was born a unity springing from their common commitment to turn the world Godward. It was their first and last meeting. Remo told Buchman, "I am going to live for Moral Re-Armament and the future of my children." As the train left, he said to his friends, "Let's go home. My heart is at peace. I am now at peace with God. I have accepted His calling to do what I must in this world."

He had only two more weeks to live. During that time many people came to his home to see him. Many changed. One of them was Raffaele D'Angelo, a Communist comrade who had fought with Remo in the partisans during World War II. He had been bodyguard to Togliatti, the head of the Italian Communist Party, when that man visited Milan. Another was La Zia. On the day Remo died she stood by his bedside. Remo was too weak to speak. He could only look at her. She said afterwards, "In that look I knew he challenged me to change. I took the decision as I stood there beside him." Since then La Zia has returned to the Catholic Church, and when Remo was laid to rest, hundreds of Communist comrades, men who long since had left their faith, marched in procession with their trade union banner to the church and took part in the service.

Raffaele D'Angelo and his wife have been changing men, including former Communists. He says, "Remo Biotello gave me new hope. He carried me by his faith into a fight which I know he would have continued, shoulder to shoulder with us, had he lived. This fight leaves neither victor nor vanquished, neither hatred nor bitterness, but only the deep satisfaction of knowing that we have a part together in building a new world."

Buchman believed that the non-Communist and the Communist worlds share one failure. Neither has succeeded in creating a new type of man, free from selfishness, who is fit to carry humanity forward into the dangers and opportunities of the atom age.

Hans Bjerkholt, a founder of the Communist Party in Norway in 1923 and for thirty years a member of the National Executive, shares this view. He says, "Again and again I have sat in the Kremlin and noticed that the unfinished business there is the creation of a new type of man. We thought a change in economic conditions would produce him. Economic change, social change, political change, all are necessary, but none by itself frees a man from selfishness, hate and greed."

Bjerkholt met Buchman and was convinced that he was face to face with a revolutionary, more committed than himself. After some days he said, "Is there a way out? There is. I have seen that human beings can be changed. We can find an ideology that unites everyone above class, above race. Lenin said there was no ideology above class. But he was wrong. If I can change, any Communist and any non-Communist can change. It is a hard and heavy work we have before us, but no difficulties can prevent me from doing what I know to be right."

Bjerkholt in 1961 spent months in Latin America helping to bring the new thinking and new living he had found, through Frank Buchman, to the millions of workers and peasants in the Northeast area of Brazil and in Peru.

Men like Bjerkholt responded to the friendship of Buchman which was given abundantly to all men of whatever background. He treated everyone as a royal soul and at the same time treated everyone as a man who through change could rise to greatness.

Hans Boeckler, post-war Chairman of the West German trade unions, heard of a meeting of 150 German industrialists that was being addressed by Buchman's friends. Uninvited, he went to the meeting. He said, "When I saw them all there it made me so sick I had to go out and have a beer. All the bosses were sitting listening." But when he came back after his beer he heard Buchman's friends give the same challenge to those employers of labor as they gave to the workers in the mines, the factories and the fields. Boeckler afterward came to Buchman and said, "I was convinced by the measure of the challenge you made to those employers."

Buchman did not write men off because they were royal nor write them up because they were workers. He treated them as men. When he fell suddenly ill and lay dying, Prince Richard of Hesse motored for hours to be at his side. Buchman's friendship with the family began forty-one years beforehand and lasted through the years in grey days and in gay, in bad times and in good. In the early years his visits to the Hesse family at Kronberg Castle were known as the "Buchman season."

Prince Richard sat by the bed of his old friend. The favorite psalms, the twenty-third, the hundred and twenty-first and others were read. Then Prince Richard said to his friend, "It's Richard, Frank. It's me. I am here." Buchman could not speak but he understood. Then Prince Richard said, "Frank, I am here and I am going to stay." Buchman understood, too, the pledge that those words contained.

It was part of Frank Buchman's secret that in his dealings with men so many did stay steadfast to the faith they learned from him.

SEVEN

America Needs an Ideology

Senior military men in America have realized the necessity that a nation have an ideology to match the demands of the twentieth century. One of them is an Admiral. He came many times to meet Frank Buchman and to be trained in Moral Re-Armament. On his return to Washington he was invited to speak to the men in control of the armed strength of America.

When he mentioned the word "ideology," one interrupted him and said, "What is an ideology, Admiral?"

The Admiral replied, "When I went to Mackinac I took a bottle of Scotch with me. I also took several novels to read. But I was so interested that I never opened the books or the bottle all through the week-end." Then he said, "Gentlemen, an ideology is when you stop doing a number of things that you have been doing, and start doing what you should have been doing all the time, and do it twenty-four hours a day, seven days a week, for the rest of your life."

An American General told Frank Buchman two years ago, "Our country is like a dead knight in armor. We have the weapons, but need the spirit and will to prevail."

Buchman loved his native country as she is, but fought fearlessly and ceaselessly for her to become the country she is meant to be. His conviction was that America with an ideology could set the whole world free.

Buchman brought the secret of that ideology to Americans who affected the life of their country. John Riffe, former Executive Vice-President of the CIO, was one of these men. When a Senator came to see Riffe, Riffe said to him, "Senator, tell America that when Frank Buchman changed John Riffe, he saved American industry 500 million dollars." Riffe meant that if he had continued to lead strikes to gain power and prestige rather than to better the conditions of the workers, it would have cost them in wages, as well as the country in loss of production, 500 million dollars.

John Riffe had a teen-age daughter, Joanna. Here in her own words is the way that Buchman changed her:

"There are four kids in our family. My father was Executive Vice-President of five-and-a-half million workers. But he found it much harder to handle his four children than all those workers. My father used to drink two quarts of whisky every day. He used to say that he and mother swore like troopers, fought like cats and drank like fish. They were getting a divorce. Mother was a fashion model. She used to spend an hour every day painting her face. When she decided to change, she got up and made breakfast for us every morning instead.

"Father described himself as a hard-drinking, woman-chasing poker-player. He came to realize he couldn't go to the conference table bleary-eyed and find the right thing for labor—or for management. He knew that Frank Buchman's vision that labor led by God could lead the world, was the real destiny of the workers. Mother and Dad accepted Frank Buchman's challenge. It was something to live for bigger than themselves. The divorce proceedings were called off.

"Four years ago I went to an MRA Assembly at Mackinac Island. I was against God because I was against absolute moral standards. I had to go faster and faster to get a thrill out of life. I had been given a car of my own and within two weeks I had smashed it driving too fast. I could see MRA would mean a drastic change in my way of life. I decided to leave Mackinac and go back to Washington.

"Frank Buchman asked to see me. I walked into his room and before I even sat down in the chair he started talking to me. For twenty minutes he blazed at me with the facts of how I had been living.

"Then he said, 'Is what I say about you true?' I was shaken—but I was stubborn and I answered, 'No.' Then he literally shook with the strength of his feelings. 'I may have the wrong details,' he said, 'but I have the right girl, the right diagnosis and the right cure. You are the girl, the diagnosis is that you are sex mad, the cure is Jesus Christ. Jesus just exactly suits, saves and satisfies us sinners.' Then he said it again, 'Jesus just exactly suits, saves and satisfied us sinners.' I knew it was a reality in his own life. He was satisfied in his heart—a satisfaction I longed for.

"Then he looked at me and said, 'Would you like to have guidance?' I replied, 'No.' There was a long silence in the room. Then he said, 'Well, during that quiet time my guidance was that you will stay, that you will change and that you will be mightily used.'

"Then he said, 'Would you like to pray?' 'No,' I said,

'I don't want to pray.' So he prayed—'Our Father which art in Heaven'—and went through the Lord's Prayer. By the time he had finished I knew that my life would never be the same again. He had actually cared enough to speak straight to me—the straightest anybody had ever spoken to me. It was the turning point in my life. It is useless to tell a rebel to be good. It takes a passion to cure a passion. Frank Buchman lived a quality of life that brought a cure.

"We began to be honest at home about everything in our lives that had not been right. It made our family new. We kids were no longer afraid of Dad. We realized America needed what we needed—to be honest and to live straight."

John Riffe first met Buchman when he was West Coast Director for the United Steelworkers. He and two organizers, Jack Flannery and Bob Shippey and their wives, motored from San Francisco to Brookdale Lodge in the Santa Cruz Mountains for a week-end with Buchman. They had supper together at a table beside the brook which runs through the dining-room of the lodge.

After supper Buchman's friends, including representatives of management, got together. They spoke of what was needed to bring unity to America. One man told how to get guidance from God and to write it down.

However, neither Buchman nor Flannery was there. Flannery had headed for the bar across the street—an old habit of his. But there was a difference. Buchman was beside him —one foot on the rail—drinking ginger ale. John Riffe always referred to this care of Buchman for Flannery as a turning point in his own life.

Next morning, an hour before breakfast, Buchman knocked on the Riffes' door, with a tray of coffee. "I thought you might like a cup of coffee to drink while you are having your quiet time," said Buchman. "It was just as if we had been having quiet times all our lives," John Riffe said.

At breakfast Jack Flannery asked Frank, "Do you think God knows who I am?" Frank replied, "Jack, God has your name written down in His book up there. He told me so Himself." Flannery never forgot that.

A few weeks later the men met again at Lake Tahoe. Buchman placed John Riffe in the care of the young son of a prominent West Coast business family. This son, Bill, had been a playboy. He did not talk hours or wages with John. He took him fishing. They were up at five and Bill cooked Riffe some bacon and eggs. Out on Tahoe Lake in the dawn hours Riffe did some thinking. Bill told him how he had changed. Riffe's catch was two small fish. But Bill had begun to catch Riffe.

That evening at dinner John noticed the two young women serving at table. "Who are they?" asked John. "They are Bill's sisters," said Buchman. John was amazed. "Those girls serving me!" he exclaimed. "Why, we are planning to strike their father's business!"

The next week-end he was back with more organizers and a load of fruit and vegetables as his contribution.

The third week-end he reported the settling of a bitter strike against Bethlehem Steel at Alameda. Riffe said it was the best contract the steelworkers had yet had on the West Coast. The strategy for the settlement had come to him in his morning guidance. "He taught me to go for what was right, not who was right," said Riffe.

In 1953 John Riffe sent a telegram to the President of the Lehigh Valley Newspaper Guild (CIO) in Allentown, Pennsylvania, Frank Buchman's home town, in which he said:

"Frank Buchman has for years led the way in the fight for moral standards and social justice in the life of nations. I have known Frank Buchman since 1940, and I count his influence on my life the deepest stimulus to sound labor thinking that has ever come my way."

Riffe and his family took time every morning to get guidance together. They wrote their thoughts down as Frank Buchman had taught them to when first they met. This habit became the cornerstone of the family's life and of John's labor leadership.[1]

The thoughts Riffe recorded one morning shortly before he died summarize his experience: "This old world is in such a man-made mess that man's mind cannot solve the problems. I know it. We must all listen to a Higher Authority than man to learn how to change, first ourselves, then others, and so find our way out of the mess. I believe from the bottom of my heart that only the Voice of God can lead us on the Right Way."

Buchman's friends included great pioneers of American management as well as labor. Firestone, Edison and Ford, all knew him well and all were deeply influenced by him.

Henry Ford never gave nor left Buchman money. But he offered generous hospitality to Frank Buchman and his friends. "We had that kind of friendship," said Buchman of the Fords, "where money was neither expected nor given."

Through the war years, Ford helped MRA during the crucial ideological battle for production. He used to come in the evenings and would act as usher at the meetings and plays being given to workers and management. Often he invited industrial friends to his Greenfield Village theatre to

[1] The story of Riffe's life is told in *John Riffe of the Steelworkers*, by William Grogan (Coward, McCann, New York, 1959).

meet Buchman. He used to say, "Put that man Buchman in a forest and he'll change the trees." He caught something of this spirit himself. Once he told Buchman, "Since you came here last year, nineteen of my managers have been saved from divorce as a result of what I learned from you. I have been in their homes, and I know." In 1942 the Fords suggested to Buchman that he should start a training center on Mackinac Island to make this new thinking normal in America.

Those who knew Henry Ford will remember how reluctant he was to use the telephone. But one Sunday afternoon he called Buchman and asked if he would like two boxes for a concert that evening. Buchman accepted. He went to the gatekeeper at Dearborn to pick up the tickets. The gatekeeper said no tickets had been left, but he would call the house. He did so. Word came that Buchman was to go up to the house.

When he arrived, Henry Ford took him to the farthest drawing-room and lit a fire. He said that his doctor advised an operation and what did Buchman think about it? They talked for about an hour and a half. It seemed the right thing to do. Then they went to the next room and Henry Ford lit another fire. He said one of the things on his mind was his will. He had not made one and he wished to do so. He went over all the things he had in his mind. He decided what he wanted that will to be. Then he made it.

Henry Ford told Buchman that evening that he had nobody to look after Mrs. Ford when he went to hospital. So Dr. Buchman agreed to look after her. He left late at night.

Next day, in the morning, Henry Ford attended to his affairs and in the afternoon went into hospital. That day

Dr. Buchman called for Mrs. Ford and took her to Greenfield Village. They had their pictures taken in the tintype gallery.

Later, when Dr. Buchman lay ill himself, Mr. Ford telephoned to Saratoga to be sure his friend was rightly cared for and progressing.

When Ford died, Buchman was in Europe. He asked two friends to call and leave a message for Mrs. Ford. They went immediately, the night after his death, to the gate of "Fairlane," the Ford home, to leave Buchman's message. The watchman called the house and, although she was seeing nobody, Mrs. Ford asked them to come up at once. Her first words were, "How is Frank Buchman?" She wanted to know all the latest news of him and of the advance of Moral Re-Armament across the world.

Henry Ford saw in MRA a force to translate private moral convictions into public policy. In a statement to the Press he declared, "Moral Re-Armament gives me hope for the future of my country and the world because of the results I see being achieved."

Another true friend of Buchman's was Joseph Scott of Los Angeles. He was nominated America's most outstanding Catholic layman in the year 1936. He was a well-known lawyer. Three Popes honored him. Between 1926 and 1938 he spoke at five International Eucharistic Congresses. He founded the Knights of Columbus in California and was chosen to nominate Herbert Hoover for the Presidency of his country. Millions knew him affectionately as "Mr. Los Angeles."

Joe Scott's faith was deep and simple. As a young man he left his Irish home and sailed to the New World. He often said, "I remember kneeling on the deck of the ship as we passed the Statue of Liberty and thanking God for coming to this country. My little mother let me go, and I shall never forget her. I shall see her again in Heaven as surely as I see you talking to me here."

One of Scott's sons was a priest. He suddenly died. Buchman read the news and at once went to Scott's home. Scott opened the door. Buchman simply took hold of the hand of the old Irishman and said, "Joe, God knows best." That was all. Tears rolled down Scott's face. That incident riveted a comradeship unbroken until Joe Scott died in 1958 at the age of ninety.

In the last three years of his life Joe Scott traveled over 35,000 miles in Asia, America and Europe to advance the work of Moral Re-Armament. Joe said to an international audience in Europe, "The world is full of men who are bitter, who are creating a world without God. In the present struggle of ideologies Frank Buchman is meeting the issues head on. As we stand at the crossroads of history there is only one answer and Frank Buchman has got it."

Joe Scott was at the Pasadena Station early one morning in 1956 to welcome Buchman to California. "Frank," he said, before Buchman had even stepped from the train—"I'm glad you've come. We need you. You have come to the land of Sodom and Gomorrah."

Frank Buchman liked to recall the story of the time he introduced Joe to a French Cardinal at tea. As tea was being offered Joe said to the Cardinal, "This reminds me of the Irishman who was asked by his hostess, 'Do you feel like a cup of tea?' 'Hell, m'am,' replied the Irishman, 'Do I look like a cup of tea?' "

It was the same Cardinal who said, "MRA is a crack of the

whip for Christians who have forgotten their mission, and offers a positive alternative to sincere Marxists."

Scott often told his friends, "Frank Buchman is not a controversial figure. He is like St. Francis of Assisi."

In 1955 Joe Scott flew from Los Angeles to Washington for an Assembly of Moral Re-Armament which brought together leaders from Washington and every continent. Joe addressed this assembly:

"The outlook in the world is blacker than it has been in my long years. We can build an atom bomb, but never have I seen so much scepticism, so much cynicism, so much bitterness, so much despair and such inadequate preparation for the future. The only adequate answer to the hate in the world is Frank Buchman's philosophy of Moral Re-Armament."

The same year Joe Scott, on Buchman's initiative, led a force of two hundred from twenty-eight nations to the Philippines. Joe introduced officials of the Japanese Government to President Magsaysay—the beginning of an historic reconciliation. A Manila paper commented: "Joseph Scott, eighty-seven years, strong in the faith of his fathers and his family—Catholicism—gave a stirring message on the impact Moral Re-Armament has on every religion—and in his Catholicism, the power to deepen and strengthen that faith in his life."

When Frank Buchman died, another of Joe Scott's sons, Monsignor George M. Scott, responsible for thousands of waterfront workers in Los Angeles and elsewhere, cabled: "I share with you greatest sorrow in the death of Dr. Frank Buchman. God grant eternal rest to his gentle soul. Lifelong friends like my beloved father Joe Scott will welcome him home with open arms."

Frank Buchman wrestled unendingly with heart and mind to find new ways of putting old truths so they could reach modern millions. The use of the theatre, the screen and television struck him as of importance without limit in changing history. Stars like Muriel Smith were won by his faith. Muriel Smith, the original Carmen Jones on Broadway, and the star of the opera *Carmen* at the Royal Opera House, Covent Garden, London, gave up her contracts and has been giving her talents and time to make films like *The Crowning Experience.*

Muriel Smith expressed her experience in words which have become a charter to her people:

"Born and raised with the race question in America, I have through my life and through my career tried to bring an answer to this problem. The results were ineffective and bordered on disaster. Then I met the force of Moral Re-Armament and discovered that the answer to that great wound in this nation could begin in my heart and in my life. It meant I had to be honest about my past, clarify my motives, and strike out with no thought of personal gain or ambition, with the love for the world that comes when we surrender our wills to be wholly committed to the power of God.

"What can I do, I asked myself, to bring the answer to the American Negro? To the American people? How can I help to make a positive out of a situation which has turned into one of the least attractive aspects of democracy? Could the lessons of slavery be used to help men? We have given our nation and the world the music of our spirituals out of that suffering. Is there something else we might give?

"There must be no hold-back because of old patterns of bitterness and hatred which have caused so much division in our country. The ideology of Communism grows on these weaknesses. The ideology of Moral Re-Armament teaches us how to heal them. When we allow our lives to be ruled by our passions, we become unwittingly the tools of men whose purpose is to control the world by any means. The end of this is slavery.

"The historical past of my people and their emergence from the bonds of slavery are on the records of history as one of the great miracles of this age. We are equipped to understand the meaning of slavery. We know what is the real meaning of victory through persecution.

"I implore you in this hour of great urgency in the free world to accept this ideology of Moral Re-Armament and use it to cure the sickness of our nation. Division can only reproduce the same conditions of slavery, but this time it will be on a global scale. Before we Americans are free to speak to the world we must be free to speak to our neighbors.

"Why do we, through the unhealed hurts of the past, permit ourselves to be used to create again the same human dilemma when there is an answer? The issue is not color, it is character. The choice is Communism or Moral Re-Armament.

"The struggle of my people has been for full participation in the affairs of our nation. This is the time to take the offensive with the ideology of Moral Re-Armament which alone can achieve that goal. We have been prepared by history for the supreme part in this our nation's task in setting the whole world free."

Muriel Smith has told how she attracted the attention of many men. She says that Buchman noticed this. When they got talking he said, "Muriel, watch those eyes." Those four words, said without heat, but with strength to the singer at the peak of her fame and fortune, made their mark.

Another of the stars who decided to join with Buchman in using her gifts to remake men and nations is Ann Buckles from Tennessee. She played in *Pajama Game* and *Mrs. McThing* on Broadway. Five days before she was due to appear in a big television show, she came to Mackinac Island not knowing just what she was coming to.

She arrived so heavily made up that if the wind blew hard, she says, parts of her face and hair would blow away. Here in her own words she describes how Buchman helped her to become different:

"I was on the point of separating from my husband, but had not told anybody about this. When I met Frank Buchman he gave me a long, quiet look and then said, 'Divorce is old-fashioned.' This startled me. It was the key to my whole life.

"I was pretending to be very modern, and saw that I was just plain lonely and frightened.

"From the first he had a tremendous vision and faith that I could be used by God to save my country, when most people just saw an over-blonde actress out for herself. He expected you to care for the world and somehow it made you want to do it.

"The first time I had tea with Frank he gave me forty-five minutes and I talked the whole time. I was self-important and full of myself. I tried to run him as I tried to run everybody. After forty-five minutes of histrionics and bad drama on my part, Frank said, 'If I have any guidance for you, I'll let you know. If I don't, it won't bother me.' And he left. At that moment I realized I had met for the first time a person who was not dominated or governed by anyone's will, but by God's. It put me exactly where I needed to be put.

"Frank was very generous. At the times when I deserved the least he gave the most. Once I had exploded about everything I felt—not so much for the sake of changing people, as expressing myself and defending my rights. I felt terrible later and very ashamed. When I went back to my room there was a beautiful arrangement of flowers with a card from Frank, 'For your splendid fight for unity. Frank.' He had a great sense of humor and mercy.

"Frank saw the worst about you, but expected and fought for the best. Many times he told me the real truth about myself and people very near to me. He spoke straight to me about one friendship that was wrong. I saw and accepted the truth completely and said, 'Yes, Frank, that's true about my friend and that is exactly the kind of person I am because that is the kind of friend I picked.' Then he said with great passion, 'But you don't want those things any more.' Then I realized the reality of change, and the possibility of change if I chose to accept forgiveness and stop doing the wrong things and start doing the right.

"At one point when I felt most discouraged about myself, I wrote to Frank Buchman saying I had failed. He wrote back: 'God is going to use you beyond your wildest dreams. It isn't what you do for Him. It's what you allow Him to do in you and through you. If we can stop limiting God by our hold-back, and even by what we think we can do, then He can make us as different as Paul was from Saul.'

"He was very straight with me about money. Money meant far too much to me. Once Frank Buchman read a letter to us about miracles happening around the world and all that God was doing. Then he said, 'That letter is full of gold. Have you got your pockets full of that kind of gold, Ann?' He challenged me as he challenged everybody who worked with him to live on faith and by prayer.

"I had guidance to give what money I possessed to help his work forward. He wrote to me: 'There is a totally new future ahead of such self-giving, which means that God has the chance to use you every hour of every day. That is the only thing now that will meet the needs of nations.'

"He had a knowledge of what the theatre could do for the whole world. Once, before we were putting on a play, he said, 'A night of real theatre. Nothing for yourself. You will give all. This must be the end of all casualness. Plays like this open hearts and fish out sound men. The stage has its place, and a vital place. Together we are going to create the music, films and theatre that will set the whole world on the right track. Create the freedom that gives you the freedom to create.'"

Buchman made friends with men and women of Hollywood and worked for years with them because he saw all they could do and be for the world. In July 1939 he spoke to Hollywood. Thirty thousand people jammed the Hollywood Bowl, fifteen thousand more could not get in. He said there to the leaders of Los Angeles and of the film industry: "Tonight is a preview of a new world. Hollywood can become the sounding board for Moral Re-Armament to the nations."

Hollywood understood. Louis B. Mayer said at the Hollywood Bowl: "Films are meant to be ambassadors in celluloid." Twenty-one years later, Jeanette MacDonald spoke of that meeting, and of a luncheon given by Louis B. Mayer for Frank Buchman, attended by 250 Hollywood personalities.

She remembers what Buchman said at that lunch. She also remembers how Mayer stood up and apologized to her for a long-standing difference between them.

Frank Buchman did not just make acquaintances. He made friends.

Joel McCrea and his wife Frances Dee, Jeanette MacDonald and her husband Gene Raymond, are among the many stars of the screen who have been Buchman's friends over the years.

Jesse Lasky was another old friend. After the première of *Freedom*, the MRA film made in Nigeria, Lasky stood for an hour with Frank Buchman in the lobby of the theatre with Joel McCrea's son, Jody. Jesse Lasky said, "I know what it takes to make a film. In this film you have done the impossible. We in Hollywood could never have done it."

Charles P. Skouras, the head of Twentieth Century Fox, was another devoted friend of Frank Buchman. Once when he came to the MRA center in Los Angeles, Buchman had had the chorus prepare special songs. As Skouras entered the great hall, voices from more than twenty countries sang the Greek national anthem. Skouras stood there and wept.

Later that evening at a duck dinner, he said to Frank Buchman, "This dinner is going to cost me five thousand dollars. I can see it coming. You must show your plays in the Carthay Circle Theatre. I will provide the theatre and all the lighting, searchlights and all." And he did it, not once, but several times over the next years.

When a theatre was needed in San Francisco in 1951, at the time of the signing of the Japanese Peace Treaty, Charles Skouras made it available. Five of the six Japanese plenipotentiaries, after a dinner given by Buchman for them, went to the theatre to see an MRA production. Their whole attitude was changed. Afterward, Robert Schuman of France said to Buchman, "You made peace with Japan two years before we statesman had the courage to sign it."

Through statesmen and actors, labor leaders and industrialists, old and young, Frank Buchman fought to help America and the world find their full destiny under God. He himself once summed up his convictions in these words:

"My deep personal wish is to have every American free under the direction of God to fight for America; so to fight that America really be free, free from the tyranny of sin, under God's direction, the unseen but ever-present Power. I wish this no less deeply for everyone in every nation. I don't want our sons, especially our fighting sons, to go about without an answer. It simply enslaves them. It is not good enough. It will drive them to the same philosophy that rules our opponents. We shall never create an inspired democracy that way. Men must learn to have a faith that will create the right revolution. If we can spread this revolution fast enough we can save America and the world. Unless we have this revolution there will be a revolution of chaos."

EIGHT

The Result is a Miracle

The art of changing men is ageless. Buchman died at the age of eighty-three. But he went to the heart and root of life with people of all ages, daily. A few months before he fell ill, he said to a friend, "Thirty-four people came to see me yesterday." He did not say it as a boast. It was his way of life. Each person who came was given the challenge and chance to become new and to take on the kind of work in life to which he had never dared to set his hand.

A young man of twenty-one, a friend of his, had this to say about him:

"The first time I met Frank Buchman he looked at my shoes. I was sixteen then. I hadn't polished my shoes that morning. They were dirty. If feet can blush, my feet were blushing. Frank Buchman looked into the distance and said, 'You have a great life's work ahead of you.' I remember the first point about polishing my shoes as well as I do the second. Frank Buchman wanted young men like me to be clean from the sole of our shoes to the top of our heads–inside and out.

"A fellow like me was beset by temptation. Frank Buchman always talked simply to me. He told me about the different stages of his own temptations as a young man–'First the look, then the thought, then the fascination, then the fall.' He taught me to turn to Christ for help between the look and the thought. He also taught me to avoid things that tempted me, like the wrong sort of books and pictures. He used to say, 'Keep wide margins. If your problem is falling over precipices, don't spend your time taking walks along the edge of the cliff.'

"One night I was praying in his room. I was making an elaborate prayer which I hoped would impress him. Then came his turn to pray. His prayer was very blunt. He said, 'O God, help this young man to stop his dirty habits. Help us to be honest. Help us to be pure–really pure. Help us to be unselfish. Yes, and help us so to love one another that we can have a party like this any time of the night or day.' That prayer got through to me, in a big way. I left the room different."

Buchman's dealing with people was down to earth and direct. A British Colonel once came to see him. He was a man of many talents, holding a high place in the War Office. He was well known in many Christian societies in England. The Colonel said, "My son is a problem. I'm busy. So are you. Come with me in a taxi to where I must go. On the way we will talk about the boy." So they went.

The Colonel said he had done everything he knew for his son. He had prayed for him. He read the Bible to him. He made him go to church. The boy was silent, sulky and full of moods and hate.

Buchman said, "Have you been honest with your son about your own life? Have you told him what you were like at his age—and what you are like today?"

The Colonel said, "That would never do. It would embarrass the boy. We don't do that sort of thing in England."

Buchman suggested that the father might be more embarrassed than the son, and that his pride meant more to him than giving the boy what would help him most.

The taxi had stopped. The clock went on. The fare went up and up. But the Colonel would not let Buchman go. At last he said, "It won't work. But I've tried everything else. I'm willing to try your way."

A few days later the Colonel came back. He was smiling. He said, "It's a miracle. I was honest with my son. He was honest with me. Everything is different. He has found faith. We have become friends." The Colonel also became a man who brought change to others, instead of being the sort of Christian that people are prone to admire—and avoid.

Some people believe that Buchman's art is too simple. It is true that he often found that the real problem in a person's life is something much more simple than he is willing to admit. When he first came to Oxford, men wanted to spend hours discussing with him their intellectual doubts. He often said, "Your problems are not intellectual. They are moral." Again and again he was proved right. He used to say, "What some people need is not a feather duster but a rotary street-broom, and some strong disinfectant."

But his surgical skill with the spirit of men was a delicate and intricate art that continued through the lifetime of those who became his friends.

The story of his faithful dealing with one of them paints this picture.

This man was at the top of his profession, but without faith. He had friends who used to say to him, "What you need is an experience of Christ." The friends were sincere. But the outcome was that the man told his secretary to say he was out when they telephoned or called. He had a happy home and was full of ambitions ripe for fulfilment.

By chance he met Buchman and those who worked with him. They did not start by talking to him about God or Christ. They spoke of the man's own profession and the things that he was doing. He became interested in the results of what he saw them doing, and at last asked them to tell him of their work.

They spoke of absolute moral standards. The man, with a university training in philosophy, said, "Oh, there is no such thing as an absolute standard." They answered, "If a standard is not absolute, then it is no standard at all."

Though he did not then admit it, he knew this was true. They suggested that he should try honestly to listen to God. He said, "I do not believe in God." Someone said, "In that case, you would not mind listening to Him, would you? Because you need not be afraid of any result."

He made the experiment. He sat quietly and asked God to speak to him. He had certain clear thoughts, the first of which was to be honest with his wife. Others concerned money, a jealousy against another member of his family which had caused division, and the fact that, in spite of looking upon himself as an idealist and better than most people, he was in truth living for himself alone, for his own success, his own satisfactions, his own security in life.

He wrote none of these things down, and when asked if he had had any guidance from God, answered, "Not a thing. It doesn't work for me."

Buchman's friends did not press the point. They said, "People who say they have no guidance when they begin to listen, often have some thought which they don't want to face. You may think it's an ordinary thought. The important thing is to be honest about it."

This was so near the mark that he went home feeling uncomfortable. At last he decided to do the things he had thought about. He became honest with his wife. Moral change had started in his life.

There was as yet no faith. But as he listened day by day, he began to get insight from God about things in his nature —bad temper, habits, deep-set ways—over which he had no control. Buchman's friends said to him, "If you put right the things you can put right, God will put right the rest." They talked about Christ to the man, now that he realized he was up against things in his own nature about which, in his own strength, he could do nothing. They told him that Christ and His power would meet a man at the point of his deepest need.

F-A-I-T-H—"Forsaking All I Take Him"—was a phrase that meant much to him at this time. Faith began for him when he found a power from outside himself to do to his character what he could not do himself. He also began to get thoughts in the early hours of the day about other people. When he acted upon them, others began to change. He was led to the conviction that there was an Intelligence outside himself which knew things about others that he did not, and which could use him to help them, if he were willing to listen and obey.

Buchman held him to simple daily discipline and to costly personal decision. He taught him to take time each morning to pray to God, then to listen to Him. "What God says to us is at least as important as what we say to Him." He had the man read the Bible to him, Old Testament and New. Passages like I Corinthians vi, verses 9–11 became familiar. "Know ye not that the unrighteous shall not inherit the Kingdom of God? Be not deceived. Neither fornicators, nor idolaters, nor adulterers, nor effeminate, nor abusers of themselves with mankind, nor thieves, nor covetous, nor drunkards, nor revilers, nor extortioners, shall inherit the Kingdom of God. And such were some of you: but ye are washed, but ye are sanctified, but ye are justified in the name of the Lord Jesus, and by the Spirit of our God."

They prayed together night and morning, quite naturally opening their hearts to God about the needs of themselves, the work of Moral Re-Armament and the world as they saw them.

Buchman also held him to being completely honest about every detail of his life with at least one other person whom he trusted. This was not just to unburden something on to somebody else. It was because the man needed to face his own need in detail so that his sense of need for God would be deepened. "A small sense of sin means a small sense of Christ."

The places in life where he had gone wrong and where God had put things right, then became his weapons in remaking other people. Frank Buchman once said to him, "You don't know what to do with your sins. I use mine. I drive them like a team of horses. They are my entry into the hearts of other people. Telling them how good I have been, and how well I have done, never impressed them much.

Telling them honestly where I have failed often helps them to be honest about themselves."

Then he added, "That doesn't mean telling everybody all about yourself all the time, in private or in public. That is wrong. Dead wrong. But you must learn to live free from the pride that is not ready to tell anybody anything about yourself if, in guidance, you see it will help him. Never tell anything to somebody else which involves a third party."

Once he saw a number of people from Australia, when this man was present. The Australians were talking about their moral difficulties. Buchman said, "Honestly, I do not know how you get into that sort of thing. I do not have time to live with dirty thoughts and dirty deeds. There are too many interesting things to think about."

The Australians became angry. They thought Buchman was making himself out to be a better man than they were. So he said, "I don't say that I am without temptation. You can't stop the crows flying over your head. But you can stop them making nests in your hair. I do say that if I am tempted, I am willing to tell the first person I meet if it is the thing that will help him most."

When the man asked Buchman how to deal with sin, he replied, "Hate it. Quit it. Be honest with somebody about it. Put right what you can. Then GROW–Go Right On Working."

This man found that he had to deal with many in the modern world whose problems were homosexual. Shame often made such people either lie or pretend there was nothing wrong with their perversion. Loneliness and bitterness were often covered by malice, wit and bravado. Cruelty sometimes walked hand-in-hand with that vice. Buchman did not regard homosexuality as a sin different in dimension from any other. He told the man, "Sin is the disease. Christ is the cure. The result is a miracle."

He had endless understanding and patience with those who wanted to find a cure to the twists in their nature. But he had small sympathy with self-styled Christians who, because they lacked the experience to bring the cure, pretended there was no sin there, only some sort of misfortune or sickness caused by the shortcomings of parents or others. "It's a denial of the power of Christ," he used to say. "They ought to read the first chapter of Romans."

One morning the man Frank Buchman was training had two clear thoughts. They were: "Live absolute purity for My sake. The heart of this revolution will be your permanent home for the rest of your life." This represented for him the same cutting of all human security which Buchman faced when he gave up his paid job. It might mean never going back to his home or his own country again. It meant being ready for anything and everything God demanded. The man was not ready.

He told nobody of the thoughts he had had. He went on as before, but with the secret resolve that he was unwilling to go as far as that.

At the same time, in order to make up for the guilt in his heart because of his compromise, he began to pay particular attention to Buchman, to flatter and to praise him.

The treachery of Judas shows itself in either kissing or killing the character of the person you have wronged or whose challenge you have refused.

Buchman sensed instantly the compromise in this man. He knew too that, because he had somewhere refused to obey God and rely on Him, the man would turn more and more to somebody like himself for correction, direction and comfort in life. From one day to the next Buchman bolted and barred every door and window in their relationship. Nothing that the man could do was right. Publicly and privately, in and out of season, he was rebuked and assailed. Buchman was determined that the man should turn to God alone and to no human authority for his foundation in life.

Once, at a meal to which many important guests were invited, the man was asked to sit at Buchman's table. When Buchman arrived and saw him there he at once and in a loud voice, said, "Take him away. I will not sit down at table with him. I do not want him among these people."

This incident was typical of the relationship between them at that time, and things continued so for nearly four years. When once or twice they had guidance together, Buchman's conviction for him came in the verse of the old hymn, repeated again and again—

> Nothing in my hand I bring,
> Simply to Thy Cross I cling;
> Naked, come to Thee for dress;
> Helpless, look to Thee for grace;
> Foul, I to the fountain fly;
> Wash me, Savior, or I die.

Once the man asked, "How long shall I go on in this state of darkness and despair?" Buchman replied, "I just don't know. It's your decision, not mine." The man still refused to be honest.

At last he decided that, no matter what it meant, if he spent the rest of his life washing dishes or scrubbing floors, he was nevertheless going to do what God asked, to live purity, and to make the heart of the battle for a remade world his lasting place.

He got honest with friends about the guidance he had had and had refused four years earlier. On his knees with them he accepted God's task and calling for his life in its fullness.

This decision was at once put to the test. He was at the time with fourteen other people. A telegram came from Buchman inviting all the others, but not him, to come to an Assembly in Switzerland.

The man went back to his own country. He began to change people in a way that worked. God was using the new steps he had taken. After two months an invitation came to him from Buchman. The man went. Buchman was polite, but no more than that. The barriers were still up. He wanted to see whether the man really meant to live his decision or whether he still depended on the favor of any living man.

After some weeks, as he was walking along a passage, the man felt a hand on his arm and Buchman's voice said at his side, "Just like old times, isn't it?" That was all.

From that time, and for many years, the men worked as one together. But there was God in the center of the relationship and no false loyalties to man. Buchman firmly held everybody to the knowledge that any relationship with any other person that is more important to you than your relationship with God–or theirs–has something wrong with it. He fought tooth and nail, hammer and tongs, hell for leather, the thing in people which led them to try to put a wrong dependence on him or on any other living man.

Some time after these things happened, the man told Buchman, "I love my wife and children very much. But I see that my relationship with them is the root of the craving which all my life has made me lust for human affection and appreciation, and dread blame. It has been a mainspring of the force of ambition in me. For years I have wanted success because of the human praise it brings. I have longed to have one place in the world where, even if everything went wrong, I could still be sure of the comfort of human care. I have made my home that place. So my wife and I and our children have put ourselves first, before God, in each other's lives. We have not held each other to the highest at times when it might really hurt. We have robbed ourselves of the Cross. Now we have talked things over. We have decided to be as straight with each other and with all men as you have been with us. That is how we are going to live from now on."

Frank Buchman was silent. Then he said, "You know, I have had to be ready to risk every relationship in life, day and night, seven days a week, for the last forty years. Otherwise our work would not be where it is in the world today."

For him the meaning of absolute love was a freedom from any fear in his approach to people. He felt that anything in a man's life which comes before his relationship with God is sin. Christ talked about this when He spoke of people putting wife, parents or children before Him.

One morning Buchman asked whether some action he had taken was right or wrong. After the man had given his opinion, Buchman said, "You will always give me the correction I need, won't you? I am just like everybody else. I need correction every day in my life, but too few people have the care or common sense to give it me."

When, some months later, the man told Frank Buchman that the decisions he and his wife had taken had deepened and widened and strengthened their love and life together,

Buchman asked about two people who had hurt his family and said, "Are you bitter?" The man answered, "Bitter? Why, they are two of my best friends. Of course I am not bitter."

"Well, think about it," said Buchman.

The man went away and thought. He had the clear guidance next morning: "It is as if you had been kicked by a horse. You think you are not bitter about the horse. But you take good care not to walk behind it again. Fear. Fear. You are afraid they may say or do something that will hurt your wife and family again. Fear lives next door to hate. Put it right with them." The man wrote to the people and put things right. The letters brought deep change to these people.

Later still, when they were talking together, this man repeated to Buchman the verse which meant so much to him, "The blood of Jesus Christ His Son cleanseth us from all sin." "What does it mean to you?" asked Buchman. The man said, "I believe that Christ died for me, as He died for everyone, and that if we turn to Him He washes us from the stain of our sin and forgives and cleanses." "That's true," said Buchman, "But yours is still a limited experience."

He helped the man to see that Christ was able not only to clean him from the guilt of sin but to free him permanently from its power. This man had looked on his nature as an ugly rock on which seagulls had roosted, and left their mark. He hoped that as years went by the rock would become more shapely and less foul. He learned that, though there was some truth in this picture of growth in God, the deeper truth was that his nature was and ever would be the same ugly, filthy rock—that he would have to live with it all his days, and that all his days, moment by moment, everlastingly,

Christ was there ready with His love to change his motives into His own ways, to use and arm and lead and bless him.

He told Buchman it was to him like an endless stream flowing over a dirty doorstep. Buchman had him repeat the verse:

> Plenteous grace with Thee is found,
> Grace to cover all my sin.
> Let the healing streams abound;
> Make and keep me pure within.

Buchman said, "To me those last six words are the finest in the English language."

He believed that God could change the furniture of a man's heart, mind and will in a moment. He also believed that it was normal friendship to help those around him find a deeper knowledge of God year by year. Those who think he oversimplified issues in men and nations do not understand the years of time in mind, heart and body that he gave to ordinary men and to those who led the millions. They oversimplify who do not know the art of changing men.

You could not build friendship with Buchman by trying to do what you thought would please him. He fought strongly, with a fierceness that seemed unreasonable but which worked, against the weakness in those who tried to put their trust in him as a man. But if you were giving everything in the battle to remake the world you found yourself in natural and spurring comradeship at his side. He believed this to be the normal link of all who love God. You could not earn his friendship. He gave it freely to fighting hearts around him. Right or wrong, he would say what he felt, and expected all to do the same.

"Salted with the fire of the discipline" was a phrase he

loved and repeated. He quoted William Penn's words that ring down the ages: "Men must choose to be governed by God, or they condemn themselves to be ruled by tyrants." He knew this to be true not only for nations struggling to keep their freedom, but also for every man who wants to be free from the tyranny of dictatorship in the home, or the thraldom of defeat by vice or habit.

He wanted all men to learn to live like sons of God, and poured out his life to win that glorious liberty.

NINE

Cabinets Must Learn this Art

At the time of the Troubles in Ireland, a priest said, "Man is half beast." A diplomat replied, "Yes. And the beast is the half I like the best." He meant that few beasts behave as badly as man when man makes up his mind to behave badly. If you look at the folly and cruelty of today's world, it is hard to disagree with the diplomat or the priest. But human nature can be changed. Anybody, if that is what they most want to do, can change the most difficult person they know. The art of changing people had been lost in the modern world. That is why the modern world has lost its way.

There are three ways of looking at human nature. One is to make the best of it as it is and assume that it is the raw material of life which cannot be altered. That is what most people in the free world do today. In these circumstances, if you expect the worst, you are seldom disappointed. Faith today has become irrelevant to the everyday needs of so many people in positions of responsibility because they do not expect faith to change men.

Another way of dealing with human nature is to exploit it. All materialists, whether of the Right or the Left, do this. For example, the Communists, all over the world, use vanity, fear, ambition, lust, greed to control the life of men who control the life of nations. And if the control breaks down, they do not hesitate to use force, or to destroy life. The end, they say, justifies the means and men are only of value in so far as they are means toward the triumph of world Communism. If they cannot be bribed or forced to play their part, then they must be liquidated.

The third way of tackling human nature, Buchman's way, is to change it. It moves faster and lasts longer than the materialist method. The furniture of a man's heart and life can be changed in an instant. It is also realistic. Nobody is more filled with fantasy than the man who believes you will see the world different without dealing with human nature. Buchman told the truth when he said: "Unless we deal with human nature thoroughly and drastically on a colossal scale, nations must still follow their historic road to violence and destruction." He also said that Cabinets to govern successfully must learn the act of changing people. And the onrush of events makes it clear to all except the most selfish, or the most foolish, that unless free men can show that human motives are being changed on a colossal scale, Communism or atomic war will become inevitable.

Two points are clear: (1) We cannot expect others to be what we ourselves are not. The world is full of reactionaries who expect situations and nations to become different, but are unwilling to become different themselves. Buchman fearlessly held everyone to the truth that if he listened to God,

God would tell him where to make a start in his own life. When he had made that start, God would show him the place in another man's life where change could begin, and how to help the other man to make that beginning. (2) If we really want to see somebody else become different, we have to put the changing of that person first in our lives. We need to learn to read men like a page of print. It takes time. The Communists study men. In the Kremlin today there is a file with the details of the characters, the strengths, the weaknesses, of all people of influence in the free countries of the world. They study people in order to control them. Years ago Henry Drummond pointed out that many men study men for some personal motive. "The lawyer does it for gain, the artist for fame, the actor for applause, the novelist for his profession. When men study human nature for their own sake, for filthy lucre's sake, shall there be none to do it for man's sake, for God's sake?"

Buchman believed that all who wanted to change men for the sake of the men themselves, for the sake of the future of the world, and for the sake of God, should be ready to give adequate time each morning to the discipline of studying men under the direction of God. Almost every morning of his life he was awake at four. He believed that prayer moves the Hand that moves the world. It is in the hours of disciplined, sacrificial prayer that there comes that arresting "tick," that unexpected but illuminating thought, which, when acted upon fearlessly, may prove to be the key to another man's life. God does the work, but man has to work too. And we see moral miracles in other men's lives when we ourselves pay the price in the discipline and passion of our own.

Many years ago Buchman prayed to become super-sensitive to the needs of other people. He said later, "Sometimes I wish I had never prayed that prayer. If you want to be used to change other men, it means a care for them so deep and sensitive that when the other fellow has a hole in his shoe, your own foot feels the cold."

There are no rules to be followed in changing men. But through the years of experience, certain lessons have been learned which are true for everybody.

Don't be a bore. Some people try to shift a man's will before they have earned his interest or his friendship. They are far more interested in what they are going to say to him than in what he will say to them. But this was never so with Frank Buchman. He said, "You must learn to be silent in seven languages. People talk too much. That's not the way to win people. Often the best thing is not to say anything. You may know all about it, but don't dare to say one word till they tell you. Verse 1, chapter 1 of changing men is when somebody tells you something he has never told anyone else before about himself."

If you went to see Frank Buchman after having talked with another man, his question always was: "What did he say to you?" Never, "What did you say to him?" At the same time, he never wanted to hear anything the other man had said which was in the nature of a confidence. He trained those around him never to break a confidence.

He had little patience with bores who think that giving truth by itself is enough. He was fond of the story of the Colonel who saw the soldier firing at a distant target. The Colonel said, "Are you hitting the bull's-eye?" The soldier turned around and with a broad grin replied, "I don't know, sir, but they sure leave here with a helluva bang." He also used to say, "It's no use throwing eye medicine out of a fifty-story window on to the crowd below and hoping that a cure will be brought." He believed in an intensive preoccupation with the needs of the individual and trained others to spend enough time thinking and praying so that at the right time, and in the right way, the right thing could be said which would help the other fellow to change the direction of his life.

Don't be superficial. Many people spend hours discussing intellectual doubts and difficulties with the other person. Nothing happens. The real need of the man is missed. And of course those who have decided to live in defeat are often most proud of the intellectual doubts and difficulties which they have created to make themselves feel comfortable in doing what they know they should not do. Drummond once began a lecture in Edinburgh, "Gentlemen, I must ask the forbearance of the men here tonight who are in intellectual difficulties if I speak to the men who are in moral degradation. It has come to my knowledge from a bundle of letters from men now sitting in this room, that there is a large number with their backs to the wall. They are dead-beat, and I shall consider their cases first."

So many people today deal with surface conditions, but lack the vision of courage to get to the root of the trouble. Once Frank Buchman was talking with a man about his difficulties. They talked for a long time. The man said, "My trouble is I want my own way too much."

"Isn't there anything else?" Buchman asked.

"No," said the other man.

Then Frank Buchman, who had thought and prayed a great deal, said quite naturally, "Isn't your trouble—?" He named in clear terms the moral problem of the man. Pride broke. The man told the truth and changed. As they walked together to the subway station after their talk was finished, the man said, "Buchman, I'd have cursed you tonight if you hadn't got at my real need."

Honesty is the key. A man who is honest about himself can be honest with the other fellow. Men who want to change other people must be willing to make the moral test and to deal with the moral weakness and defeat in other people's lives. Any who have experienced the real battle for the wills and lives of men know that ninety per cent of the cynicism, atheism and selfishness around us has its roots in low physical defeat. Impurity lies behind much of the confusion and chaos of the modern world. People refuse to believe this because they will not deal with it either in themselves or in other people.

Buchman faced the cost of it. He said not long ago, with the white heat of conviction, to people from a certain nation, "The trouble with you is you will not face the cost of your compromise." Of purity he said, "You may say that it's just a personal matter. But what is happening to the nation? They tell you that in some factories impurity is so common that it is organized among the workers and especially among the subversive groups who use it as a weapon. They know that when people's morals are confused, their thinking becomes confused. Too few try to bring a great cleansing force to the nation. What is going to happen to a nation when nobody brings a cure any more? Broken homes, unstable children, the decay of culture, the seeding plot of revolution." Then he added, "If you can get people who will live up to these moral standards, and stand for them, then you have a force, a creative something in the community with a strength that nothing will gainsay. You must have that emphasis on morals, plus the saving power of Jesus Christ. Then you experience the dynamic which is almost forgotten—the Holy Spirit Who gives the guided answer and tells you exactly what to do as a clear direct call from God."

Don't be shocked or fooled. Many children find it impossible to tell their parents the truth about themselves. They know that the parents would be shocked by it. What they do not understand is that parents who are shocked by the truth about their children, have never been really honest about themselves. If you are to change other people, you have to be ready to listen with an understanding heart to everything the other man has to tell you. Buchman used to say: "People will go to a man who understands them, but does not talk too good, nor appear too wise—a man who is honest about his own feelings. Such a man is never shocked by anything he hears because he knows what a rascal he is himself. Speak up to your own experience, but not beyond it. Don't talk to somebody about things that are not real in your own life."

Many people are fooled by the reactions of those they are trying to change. They forget that a hooked fish jumps, kicks and runs. When a person's conscience begins to wake after a long sleep, it is a painful process. So, often they begin to attack and criticize the man who they think has challenged and caused the pain. That is the time when many red herrings are produced. Sometimes Frank Buchman's own personality is criticized. Questions are asked about the way he worked and about the whole nature of Moral Re-Armament. Such questions often deliberately obscure a man's real need. Questions need to be answered, but answering questions is not always the way to meet that need.

Nobody changes until sin is dealt with, and today so many people are fooled by sinners who first of all pretend sin is not there, then pretend that it doesn't matter, and finally pretend that it is right. One example is that of the perverts. Thirty or forty years ago, men who suffered from the sin of perversion pretended that they did not. Then steadily, skilfully and successfully they put forward the theory that perversion was only some form of illness and did not affect the life of a home or a nation. Finally they boldly took the line that perverts are more able, more interesting and more natural than people who do not suffer from this particular form of compromise. Millions are fooled by it, and today it is difficult to get a good job in certain professions unless you are known to favor perversion. The deviants of yesterday have become the normal of today. And those who yesterday were regarded as normal, will tomorrow be thought of as deviants, if things go on as they are.

Commissions and committees play their part in fooling the nation by making reports on various forms of sin. But those who give evidence to such committees often do not disclose their own weaknesses. It is like asking a drunkard to give evidence about the danger of drink among drivers on the roads. He reports that the danger has been much exaggerated, that a little drink clears your mind and soothes your nerves and helps some people to drive better. So everybody feels happier, and the death toll mounts.

Don't expect that nothing will happen. So many people expect nothing to happen in the other man's life, because nothing has happened in their own. "According to your faith be it unto you." "Large petitions with you bring. You are coming to a King." Those who deal trenchantly with sin, and expect miracles, see the miracles come to pass.

Buchman took nobody for granted. He did not think that a Bishop was necessarily more free from sin than a bartender. For him, sin was sin, whether in a king or a coal miner. Once he was talking to the Prime Minister of a great country and the word "sin" was mentioned. The Prime Minister's wife said, "Oh, Dr. Buchman, don't use that word, I do dislike it so much." "I'm sorry," said Buchman. "Call it anything you please. Call it rheumatism if you like." "Oh, don't call it rheumatism, Dr. Buchman," said the lady, "I am full of rheumatism."

Buchman used to say that sin binds, blinds, deadens, multiplies.

Sin binds. Men start by saying they are free to do as they please. They start doing as they please. They use their brain to argue their conscience to death. Presently they find they are prisoners to the habit which they first thought they could control, but which now controls them. "Sow a thought, reap an act. Sow an act, reap a habit. Sow a habit, reap a character. Sow a character, reap a destiny."

Sin blinds. Men and nations no longer see any difference between right and wrong. There is no black or white to them, but only a dull, dirty grey. General Ho Ying-chin, the last Prime Minister of the mainland of China before its six hundred million people fell to Communism, says, "We never saw what was happening. We loved our country greatly, but we loved our mistresses more. We did not realize till too late that they were Communist." People used to say, "Love's blind, but the neighbors ain't." That is true of democracy today. Democracy is as strong as the character of those who speak in her name, and free men are blind to the fact that the way they live shouts louder to the world than the fine speeches their representatives make at the conference tables.

Sin deadens. The man who lives with himself at the center long enough becomes dead to anything, or anyone else in the world, but the big "I" which runs him. He is apt to need women, drink, sleeping pills to lull him to sleep, pep pills to wake him up, overdoses of nicotine and other stimulants to keep him going. He becomes a walking corpse, but doesn't know it. He is also a killer. For when enough men like this live in a community, the strong man steps in and tyranny takes over. It is men spiritually dead in this way who acquiesce in the false alternative: Communism, or atomic war.

Sin multiplies. It is never a private matter. It passes like disease from man to man and nation to nation. Films, radio, television, press, books, carry the defeat in the heart of one life into the lives and hearts of millions. The problem is made glamorous. Nations decay in character and call it progress.

But there is an answer to sin. Confusion comes from compromise. Clarity comes from change. "Sin is the disease. Christ is the cure. The result is a miracle," said Buchman. "It ought to be enough to get a quick picture of sin and then move on. People ought to be so sensitive that they respond immediately and change. Be sure there is no minimum emphasis on sin. Make it maximum. But then quickly make the adjustment. Change, unite, fight. That is the natural sequence."

It was Frank Buchman's belief that everybody who wanted to be a remaker of men and nations should in the first waking moments of every day, move out of themselves into Christ and then out to others and live out to others all through each moment of every day.

Don't leave off just when things have begun to happen. Buchman believed that God's plan for every life was far bigger and better than anybody's plan for his own life. He was not interested in making men good for the sake of being good, but in helping them to be guided by God to play their full part in bringing revolution to the whole world. He had no patience with those who believe that change means putting on the brakes, turning off the engine and letting the air out of the tires. He believed that a personality cleansed and guided by God would go faster and further than before, but in the right, not the wrong direction. He had no use for the muted personalities and modulated tones that some people think of as Christian. He said to an Asian statesman, as he went forth from Caux to his native country, "If you would save your nation, forget yourself and go all out." He was far more interested in the things a man felt God wanted him to go and do, than in the things a man felt God wanted him to stop doing, important as both points may be.

He had high vision for men and for nations. He told the Prime Minister of Japan that Japan was meant to be the lighthouse of Asia. A few days later that Prime Minister told the whole nation that this was the aim of his government. He told Archbishop Makarios, President of Cyprus, that Cyprus should be the golden bridge between Greece and Turkey, Europe and Africa. The Archbishop made that the theme of his first public statement after his country became free. And on the day of Cypriot freedom, the President and Vice-President of the island sent the first Cyprus flag to leave their country to Frank Buchman at Caux as a sign of their thankfulness for what he and his work had done for their country.

He expected everyone to deal with others in such a way that nations felt the influence of their lives upon their affairs.

Eight Japanese came to see Buchman. They came from

some of the leading families in Japan. As soon as they had sat down to lunch, Buchman said, "What is your plan for Japan?" There was silence.

Then Buchman said, "Are you united?" Again there was silence.

Buchman went on, "I know you have done some good work in Japan, but what's happening to your nation? It's slipping fast."

Buchman then asked them what was the real problem in Japan. "Communism," they answered.

"It's corruption and mistresses," said Buchman. "Will you tackle these issues in your leaders and in your nation? I love Japan, and I am concerned about what's happening there."

The Japanese left the room. They were honest with each other. There had been jealousy between them, and impurity, and bitterness. They became united, faced where their nation stood and asked God how to bring an answer swiftly. Within three days they had written a play which they called *Shaft of Light*. It was so direct that they were afraid of what men would do to them and their children if they put it on. They read it to Buchman. He said, "Go where the stones are rough. People may want to shoot you, but you will save your nation—and future generations will be grateful."

A month later the play was staged in Tokyo, 400 yards from the Parliament building. It shook and shocked Japan. A top security man seeing the plot unroll, with its tale of bribery in high places and Communist mistresses attached to Cabinet Ministers, said, "It is exaggerated. You can't continue with this play. It is dangerous." A few days later he came back to them. "I was wrong," he said. "I have had it investigated. I found that everything in the play is true. The situation is deadly serious. Here is the answer." Members of the Cabinet, leading industrialists and trade unionists came to see the play. Television took it to the whole nation.

The Prime Minister sent for the men who had seen Buchman. They told him the facts about Japan and about his own Cabinet. They challenged him to clean things up. He said, "You are the only people who love our country enough to tell me the truth. Go on talking to me like this. The door is always open to you." Men changed through *Shaft of Light* were a major factor in holding Japan steady when Communism struck through students' riots in 1960.

For Buchman such direct dealing was all in the day's work. He expected everybody to be direct and clear in their dealings with other people. For him this was the normal life of a revolutionary. He believed that everybody could do the extraordinary thing if they were guided by God. As he stood once on the rolling hillside in Pennsylvania beside the family grave, where he now rests, all he said to his friends was, "I have been wonderfully led." And his belief and experience was that for all who wished to be led by God, treasures lay waiting beyond their dreams or their imagining.

TEN

Future Leadership

Nearly a quarter of a century ago Frank Buchman said, "If I do not train many others to do what I have been doing better than I do it, I shall have failed." For many years he worked to make himself dispensable. This was the way in which he differed from so many other human "leaders."

He said once, "I am going to promise you one thing—I am not turning back. I am not turning back no matter who does, no matter what it is going to cost. I do not want you to come along just because I am here—that isn't it. That would be a poor revolution. That would be a poor fellowship. Let us for a moment see a picture of the Cross of Christ, and let me say, if you join in this great crusade you will get the way of the Cross. I am not going to lure you by hopes of material success. I am not going to lure you by saying you are going to be heroes . . . It is a personal experience of the Cross. It is not I, but Christ. It is not I at the head, but Christ who leads."

Buchman meant this. He lived it. He held people to working together and seeking from God what was right. Few things made him more angry than the desire of some people to find in him their authority or to have him tell them what they should do. That is why surmise about the successor to Buchman or the future leadership of Moral Re-Armament is fruitless. The work will be carried forward in the future as it has been for many years past, by men who have learned to live free from jealousy and ambition and to go all-out and all together for the right as God gives them to see the right. Why should anyone or any group be chosen to give the sort of "leadership" Buchman always refused to give in his lifetime?

In the months following Frank Buchman's death, leaders of the nations and other people poured into Caux in numbers seldom equalled even while he was living.

One of the leaders was U Nu, Prime Minister of Burma. He said strong things about the need of the swift growth of Moral Re-Armament. He was sure that man would destroy himself unless he made use of Frank Buchman's secret to answer the problems of this age.

But the way in which the Prime Minister dealt with the needs of the ordinary man shows how he himself had begun to learn the secret of Buchman's life.

One of the last things Buchman had said to U Nu was, "You must learn to read men like a book."

At Caux in September 1961, five weeks after Buchman's death, U Nu found himself sitting at table next to a docker from Brazil. The docker told how he had begun to change, losing his love of violence and taking up the struggle to remake the world. "I was a drunkard," he said, "and this nearly destroyed our home."

"I used to drink far too much also," said the Prime Minister. "I began at the age of ten. Then I gave it up. But being a weak man, I took to the bottle again. At the age of twenty-six I stopped, and I can say that today I would sooner die than drink too much."

The docker talked about his hate. "Have you lost that too?" asked U Nu. "Do you feel sure you are permanently free from bitterness? Not one drop left?"

With care and sensitivity he dug to the root of the docker's life, helped him to bring to the surface the causes of his bitterness and to find a cure.

U Nu said at Caux: "If we want to stop Communism taking hold of the world we must deal with corruption, bribery, drink and womanizing." He has seen the effects of Moral Re-Armament in his own country. In 1961, the Conference of the Presiding Abbots' Association, representing 75,000 Buddhist monks, spent much of its annual session on MRA and, as a result, five senior abbots joined Buchman at Caux for his eighty-third birthday. They returned determined that Moral Re-Armament shall become the national policy of their country, and today films, books and magazines of MRA are being taken by the monks into every part of Burma.

Frank Buchman's work with the ordinary man and the statesman lasts. It is true that some people slide away. There is nothing new in this. St. Mark told the story in the fourth chapter of his book. But for many the seed sown in their heart as they talked with Buchman grew and gave forth an hundredfold.

When the MRA musical play, *The Vanishing Island*, was showing in Berlin in 1956, the crowds were so great that they overflowed the Titania Palace. There were long queues standing on the snow-covered pavements. A Town Hall was hired to hold the crowds who could not get seats in the theatre.

Two nights running a Canadian noticed an old, bent, shabbily dressed man standing at the back of the crowded Town Hall. The second night the Canadian got him a chair. Afterward the old man came up to him and said, "Do you remember me?"

The Canadian searched his memory in vain. "You were here with Dr. Buchman in 1936, weren't you?" said the old man.

"Yes," said the Canadian, "I was. Did we meet then?"

"I was the elevator-man at the hotel," said the old German. He looked down at his worn clothes and shoes. "Nowadays I find it hard to get work. I am unemployed. Things are difficult here."

Slowly he took a battered wallet from his pocket and, after searching for a little, handed the Canadian a visiting card, worn and dog-eared. On one side was engraved "Frank N. D. Buchman." On the other, in Frank Buchman's handwriting, were the words: "To Max—friend and fellow fighter. Frank."

"Every night, when Dr. Buchman came into the hotel," said the man, "he used to have a talk with me, however late it was. He would take me to his room and we would talk. He saved my home. It was breaking up because I was in the grip of drink. But Frank Buchman helped me to find faith and direction from God. He put me on the right road."

He felt in the wallet again. From it he took a fifty-mark note, almost all he possessed. He handed it to the Canadian.

"When you see Frank Buchman," he said, "will you give him this for his work. And will you please say to him: 'Max has kept the faith.'"

Buchman for years held his friends firmly to the truth that if they were not changing people they were doing nothing effective to cure a world in crisis. In 1925 he wrote an article in the *Indian Standard*. This was at a time when the early foundations of his work were being built around the world. But the principles set out in that article remained and remain the principles of Moral Re-Armament.

Here is what he said:

"There are two passages in the New Testament that illustrate just what we have sought to emphasize.

"The first is the story of the blind man whom Jesus healed. Jesus touched him the first time and when asked what he saw, the blind man said, 'Men as trees, walking.' Jesus touched the blind man the second time and then he saw 'all things clearly.'

"Many have received but the first touch—they see men as trees walking, statistics, the numbers under instruction, the numbers of men in their college or school, or the numbers that come to church, a forest of men. They see men in the mass, but fail to see 'every man clearly.' It is the need of the second touch that must be emphasized, that healing of sight that enables workers to see every man clearly, men one by one, with their individual needs, possibilities, joys, sins, successes and failures.

"The second passage is that beautiful one dealing with the meeting of Jesus and the Samaritan woman at the well near Sychar. Jesus went behind all race prejudice, convention and mere form, to lay His healing hand on the sin-sick heart of that despised woman. The woman went off to the village and told the villagers to 'Come, see a man which told me all the things that ever I did.' Come, see a man who *understands*. What was the result? 'Many Samaritans believed.' And it is ever so. The world is hungry for men and women who can *understand*—men and women brave enough, tender enough, loving enough to break reserve, to push aside mere conventions and enter into the closed rooms of sin-sick hearts that they may be opened to the healing touch of Christ.

"It is not personal work that ends in points of contact but personal work that leads to change. It is that Spirit-directed contact of a live soul with a dead soul that opens the way for the living Christ to heal the sin-sick heart. It is the doctoring of souls—sin the disease, Jesus the cure, Christians the physicians, and the results miracles.

"We are in danger of not knowing the needs of men because we are not in actual touch with needy individuals. Some of us never have individuals tell us things they have never told another; men do not seek us out and confide the deepest things of their hearts. And how are we to know our failure? How are we to know we are missing the mark unless we are in constant touch with sin-sick individuals and are learning their needs from their own lips?

"I was sitting some time ago with a group of businessmen who were longing to do something for the men of their city. During the discussion one of them said, 'We don't go deep enough; we mean well but we don't get at the root of things.' He put his hand upon one of the causes of so much failure in our work. We talk of the cure before we have found out the disease and men fail to see the connection between the disease and the cure. If sin is the disease, we must deal with sin. Sin first of all in ourselves—the 'little sins' that rob us of power and that keep us from being able to go out in deep sympathy to men in sin. Ill-will toward others, jealousy, ambitious self-will, criticism–how often these creep in and rob us of power!

"And then sin in others. Our danger is that we trust to contagion to win men to Christ. We fail to get at the sin that is keeping a man from Christ. Fear often holds us. We say we are too reserved, that no one should infringe upon another's personality, and all the time there are men about us who long to share with us the deepest things in their hearts, only we repel them by our fear and lack of understanding sympathy. The woman at the well had no feeling that Jesus had infringed upon her personality when He lovingly put His finger upon the cause of her heartache.

"Men are hungry for those who *understand* and who will get behind convention and talk reality from hearts that have suffered like pains and have won, through no merit of their own but through the gracious power of a forgiving and loving Christ.

"Do we see miracles in the lives of men because of our work? If Christ has not fully satisfied us, if there is a hunger for something, we hardly know what, may it not be because we have failed to express ourselves in the lives of men one by one? We do indeed know God. We must also know men, and, for many, a life in Christ has been found to satisfy only when that life has begun to express itself in the lives of men one by one."

Remaking men was the passion of Frank Buchman's life for more than fifty years.

In 1938, when he was sixty, the Archbishop of Canterbury, Cosmo Gordon Lang, sent him a message which spoke of the great work he had been able to achieve "in bringing multitudes of human lives in all parts of the world under the transforming power of Christ."

"If you are changed," said Buchman in Sweden a few weeks later, "you naturally want to change other people. The next thing is you want to save civilization. Then you want to reach the millions out there. It is a natural program. Some of the cleverest people in the world are thinking along the line of destructive revolution, and they are already at work. Unless we and others see the bigger vision of spiritual revolution, the other may be possible. The point is: are we going to build a Christian philosophy that will move Europe? Are you the kind of Christians that can build that revolution?"

At the end of his life he closed one of his last speeches with these words: "The world is on the knife-edge of decision. We must go all out to save our nations. When men change and are gripped by the fire and passion, the purity and honesty of a moral ideology, miracles happen. The foundation is laid of a new world, not on the shifting sand of corruption and compromise, but on the rock-like character of God-directed men and nations."

Buchman had no rules in his dealings with men. His unexpected actions were sometimes the hook which drew men closer to God through the years.

Mahatma Gandhi owed much to his friend Buchman. His son Devadas told how once in London, at a time when the British scorned his father and he was being called a "naked fakir" by those who later came to grasp his greatness, Buchman invited his father and himself to lunch.

At that time Gandhi's money was short. After lunch Buchman took his friends outside, asked them where they were going and called a taxi. He asked the driver how much the fare would be and paid it. Then after another moment of thought, he tipped him too. Devadas Gandhi said, more than twenty years later, "A rich man would never have thought of doing that. A man of God would."

When the time came to make the film of Gandhi's life, Devadas Gandhi asked the Moral Re-Armament international chorus to sing as background music to it his father's favorite hymn, *Lead, Kindly Light*. He said that if all Christians had lived the way Buchman lived, the story of Asia would have been different.

Buchman expected God to do things all the time that would shake nations. He often used to say, "Expect great things from God. Attempt great things for God." At the same time he was real as rain about the power and surge of evil, in a man or in a nation.

Once one of his friends met a well-known English writer, who made no secret of his physical lust for other men. This writer was fascinated by the changed lives he saw. He half hoped, half feared he could find freedom from his hated and beloved weakness.

After a few days the writer asked Buchman's friend to dinner at a London Club, and said to him, "You know I cannot live without intercourse with men. It started when, as a child, I saw my mother lying in a pool of blood after being beaten by my father. Later a well-known novelist assaulted me. Now it is my way of life. And it is useful. It is hard to get a play on the stage today unless you practice or approve homosexuality."

Buchman's friend told the writer that he had been freed himself from impure habits and from playing around with women. He suggested that God could also free the writer. The writer, however, did not respond, so Buchman's friend dropped the subject, for he felt flattered by the writer's friendship and wished to retain it.

The following summer, Buchman returned to Britain and the writer came to see him. During a half-hour talk with Buchman and his friend, the writer did most of the talking but did not reveal his problem in words. Afterward Buchman said, "We cannot rely on that man." Sure enough, the man had fled from the city. He knew he had met in Buchman someone he could not fool. Soon the writer had launched furious attacks on Buchman in the Press.

A year later, Buchman and his friend were walking together. Buchman said, "Would you say there was any homosexuality among the men you know?" "I am sure there is not, Frank," replied his friend. "I should know if there were." "You don't think that some men dominate others and others like to be dominated? You don't think that some of you have friendships which come before your friendship with Christ?" "Oh, yes, that of course," replied the man. "but what has that to do with homosexuality?" They walked some way in silence. Then Buchman said, "Of course, you were unable to help that writer, weren't you?"

Nothing more was said. It was some years before the other man began to see what Buchman meant. Then he realized that although he had never been physically attracted to the writer he had sought satisfaction in his relationship with him as surely as if he had taken the place of one of the writer's boy paramours. The writer's friendship had meant more to him, because he had been flattered by it, than his friendship with Christ, or what the writer needed.

He then saw that he sought affection and appreciation for

himself from everybody. He came to see that every relationship in life more important to a man than his relationship with God has impurity in it. It was only when he faced this root in his nature, and found a power from Christ to cut it, that he was able to help to free men who were gripped by homosexual indulgence from its tyranny.

Buchman lived the old truth, "Hate the sin. Love the sinner." He did not close his heart to men, however wicked they might be. But he refused to lend himself to the appeasement which lowers Christ's standards to suit human compromise. He was never anti-Communist, and many Communists met and found in him a man with a wider, deeper, more effective revolution than their own.

The door of Moral Re-Armament is wide open for everyone everywhere, Russian, American, African, Chinese, Japanese, German, Dutch, Greek—all men. The door is closed to the evil in the non-Communist world, the selfishness which creates social injustice and economic suffering. It is closed to the evil in the Communist world which, in the Christmas broadcast of Radio Moscow, says: "Our rocket has bypassed the moon. It is nearing the sun and we have not discovered God. We have turned lights out in Heaven that no man is able to put on again. We are breaking the yoke of the Gospel, the opium of the masses. Let us go forth and Christ shall be relegated to mythology."

Moral Re-Armament is not an organization, a sect or a religion. It is an ideology. It is the way men live and what they live for. The Catholic priest understood this when he said: "The Church does not need Moral Re-Armament, but Catholics do."

Gabriel Marcel, the French Catholic philosopher, Member of the Institute of France, understands it. In an article in

Figaro, published January 28, 1956, he wrote: "What is Moral Re-Armament? It is not a sect; it is a leaven or a seed. Those in whom the seed has been sown are changed from within. At the same time these men and women become radiant and even in a sense radioactive. Anyone who has come in direct contact with them is immediately aware of this.

"One fact which proves the scope of MRA is that the men of the Kremlin are troubled about it. Especially at Tashkent they make many broadcasts as a warning against a movement which is undermining the very foundations of the Communist ideology.

"Indeed, what more direct opposite is there to that ideology than these sudden changes in the direction of people's lives which cannot be ascribed to any economic cause? What personally moved me the most was to hear a Muslim teacher from Algeria who was arbitrarily arrested, subjected to serious torture, then expelled from North Africa although he could have had his case cleared. In a voice shaken by emotion this man declared that after meeting the French of MRA who lived their faith and fully recognized their mistakes, he had felt his hatred vanish away and meant to work with the French to build a new Algeria. On hearing this, a leading Frenchman from North Africa came to ask his forgiveness in the name of all those who by their blindness are largely responsible for the present tragedy.

"It is a hope. Perhaps it is even *the* Hope. For without this spirit which brings men together in a complete moral transparency, there is surely no alternative to the vicious circles of deception and mutual revenge. Today from Canada to Norway, from Central Africa to Iran, from India to Japan, by this road human beings have found not only a reason for living, but the amazing happiness of giving and radiating which is the way of true peace—the living peace in the light of a brotherhood which has been regained."

Buchman believed, and his friends believe, that Moral Re-Armament is the true, traditional property of the Church.

Buchman lives. He lives for ever, not only in Heaven, but in the hearts of his friends, and in the work he began and which has girdled the globe. It is fitting to end this chapter with some of the final thoughts that came to him in Freudenstadt, where the idea of Moral Re-Armament was born and where Buchman died:

"You will be mightily used here. This is where God first talked to you about the picture of the world's problems.

His purposes will ripen fast,
Unfolding every hour;
The bud may have a bitter taste,
But sweet will be the flower.
Blind unbelief is sure to err,
And scan His work in vain;
God is His own interpreter,
And He will make it plain.

"It was wise to come at this time. God is good to us. His mercy brightens all the paths we rove.

"Make this a center for the world work. Here you will lay down your life and die. You can see large vistas from here. God's wonder-world for you."

In his will he wrote: "I wish I had silver and gold for each one, but since my resources are so strictly limited I give everything that is mine to Moral Re-Armament absolutely. I want all to feel that they have a share as they partake of the priceless boon of a new life which has come to them and to me through the Oxford Group and Moral Re-Armament.

They can best perpetuate this gift by carrying forward a philosophy that is adequate for the world crisis and that will at last bring the nations to the long-looked-for golden age ushering in the greatest revolution of all time whereby the Cross of Christ shall transform the world."

ELEVEN

Brave Men Choose

Mark Twain used to say that what troubled him in the Bible was not the parts he did not understand, but the parts that he did. That is true, for many, of Frank Buchman's work.

He undertook the task of changing the trend of his time. The head of an Oxford College said, in the summer of 1961, that people no longer discuss whether or not to live moral standards: the truth is that nowadays millions believe that neither right nor wrong exists.

In the midst of all this, Buchman for half-a-century strode fearlessly forward, proclaiming old truths in new ways, facing decadent generations with a decision to let God clean up themselves and their nations from top to bottom. He challenged the statesman and the ordinary man with standards which, if accepted, mean revolution in all they think and do. In the landslide of morality and the shifting sands of an age of license, he gave the solid rock of eternal values and truth.

Of course he was persecuted. Men with such a message have been persecuted all through the ages. Some self-styled Christians who compromise on divorce, sex, drink, gambling, money and Communism, forget that Christ was crucified by the pious of his day—not because he was wrong but because he was right. How many Christians today draw any clear moral line through a community?

Buchman never shared the views of those who present Christ as powerless to cure the sickness of sin in a man or in a continent. He felt that powerless Christians were a denial of the Master they professed to serve.

He won the loyalty and love of a host of friends. By others he was hated, sneered at, lied about, mocked and scoffed at—and he was right. Some of his enemies continued their dance of derision upon his grave. They will not disturb his rest.

Buchman was not fooled by opposition of this kind. He understood the backlash of a stung conscience and the barbs of venom from those who refuse the challenge to change. He recognized the projection that lay behind so much of the vindictiveness and malice of his enemies. Men who reserved the right to live as indulgently as they pleased, strove for years to smear the work and assassinate the character of a man who said everyone should live as God commands and as He controls. Phrases like "pacifist," "communist," "nazi," "profiteer" were flung at him. They were lies designed to keep millions from finding the truth that can make men free.

He used to say "Persecution is the fire that forges prophets. Stones of criticism are so bracing. They just set you up for the day."

His answer was the conviction that "an extreme of evil must be met with an extreme of good. A fanatical following of evil by a passionate pursuit of good. Only a passion can cure a passion. And only a superior world-arching ideology can cure a world divided by warring ideologies."

His was an heroic march at a time when moral courage is rarer than it used to be. "Unto us may grace be given to follow in his train."

The question remains, "What can we do?"

The answer is given in the final words of Buchman's last public speech, *Brave Men Choose*, given at the opening of the Caux Assembly on June 4, 1961:

"We are facing world revolution. There are only three possibilities open to us. We can give in, and some are ready to do just that. Or we can fight it out, and that means the risk of global suicide. Or we can find a superior ideology that shows the next step ahead for the Communist and the non-Communist world alike. What we shall never do effectively is to patch things up by pretending that basic differences do not exist or do not matter, nor by supposing that an ideological challenge can be met by economic, political or military means alone.

"Absolute moral standards are not just questions of individual conduct today. They are the conditions of national survival. We need to scour out the dirt in our national life, our political life, our economic life, our school life and our home life through a change in men.

"Wherever men give man the place in their lives that God alone should have, slavery has begun. 'Men must choose to be governed by God, or they condemn themselves to be ruled by tyrants.'

"There is no neutrality in the battle between good and

evil. No nation can be saved on the cheap. It will take the best of our lives and the flower of our nations to save humanity. If we go all-out for God we will win.

> Then it is the brave man chooses,
> While the coward stands aside,
> Till the multitude make virtue
> Of the faith they had denied."

At a time of crisis the only sane thing is to change people.

Buchman lived his life in the faith and experience that human nature, starting with his own, could be changed. That was the root of the answer.

When men change, national economies change. That is the fruit of the answer.

With a crescendo of changed lives, world history can be changed. That, he said, was the destiny of our age.

The world talks about peace, but prepares for war. Buchman saw that peace was not just an idea, but people becoming different, and that the true peace-makers were those willing to pay the price of it by giving their lives to bring millions under God's control. That was his life and his secret.

Go and do thou likewise.

BJ
10
.M6
H567

1962